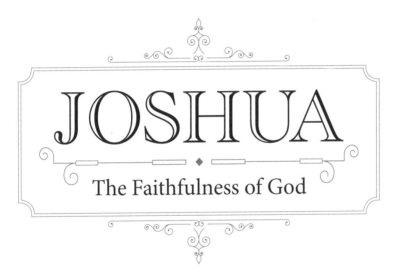

JOSHUA

The Faithfulness of God

Lifeway Press®
Brentwood, Tennessee

EDITORIAL TEAM

Robert Smith Jr.
Writer

Kima Jude
Activities Writer

Reid Patton
Senior Editor

Katie Vogel
Assistant Editor

Stephanie Cross
Assistant Editor

Jon Rodda
Art Director

Tyler Quillet
Managing Editor

Joel Polk
Publisher, Small Group Publishing

John Paul Basham
Director, Adult Ministry Publishing

ISBN: 979-8-3845-0106-0 • Item: 005848437

Subject Area: Bible Studies, Dewey Decimal Classification Number: 222.2
Subject Heading: BIBLE. O.T. JOSHUA--STUDY AND TEACHING \ LOYALTY \ GOD

Printed in the United States of America

Lifeway Christian Resources, 200 Powell Place, Suite 100, Brentwood, TN 37027-7707.

CONTENTS

INTRODUCTION

The book of Joshua is the first of the historical books in the canon. It is rich in teaching, doctrine, and history. It is prime real estate for my preaching classes at Beeson Divinity School of Samford University in Birmingham, Alabama, where I teach my preaching students to look for an Old Testament picture for every New Testament doctrine. I also invite them to look for parallel doctrines in the Old and New Testaments. It is exciting to mine the book of Joshua for these interesting bastions of truth.

While vacationing in Myrtle Beach, South Carolina, I was walking on the beach and noticed a man with a small bucket, a shovel, and a metal detector. He was using the metal detector to sweep across the surface of the beach. I asked why he was doing this. He replied, "I am searching for metal objects—things like rings, bracelets, necklaces, and watches that fall from those who walk and run on the beach. These elements become quickly buried in the sand." He explained that his metal detector would yield a ticking sound when it neared buried metal. When the sound became stronger, the treasure hunter would start digging and bring valuable commodities to the surface.

This Bible study will serve as a Christological detector for locating valuable insights about Christ illustratively, typologically, conceptually, narratively, and metaphorically throughout the book of Joshua. The book is all about Him. Jude 1:24 records, "Now to him who is able to protect you from stumbling . . ." Ephesians 3:20 states, "Now to him who is able to do above and beyond all that we ask or think according to the power that works in us . . ." It's all about Him.

Examining the Word reveals a thread of familiarity running through the book of Joshua, Hebrews, and Ephesians. These three books have the thread of inheritance running throughout their fabric. **Scripture reveals believers are heirs of Christ, who is the hero of both the Old Testament and the New Testament.** Jesus said to the Jews, "You pore over the Scriptures because you think you have eternal life in them, and yet they testify about me" (John 5:39). Ultimately, the inheritance of a Christian is not in a place but rather in a person—our inheritance is in Christ Jesus (Ephesians 2:6).

Joshua, the namesake of the book and the chosen leader of Israel, was an Ephraimite. Ephraim was one of Joseph's two sons born in Egypt of a Gentile mother, Joseph's wife. Joseph's brothers sold him (a member of their family) to foreigners, and God gave Joseph a new family. Eventually, Joseph was positioned to save his father's family from the devastating effect of famine. Joseph's father Jacob and his family eventually moved to Egypt because there was grain there, and Joseph was in charge of the grain. When Jacob was dying, Joseph brought his two sons, Manasseh and Ephraim, to see their grandfather, Jacob. Jacob not only gave Joseph's sons a prayerful blessing but also granted them a land inheritance through the process of adopting them (Genesis 48).

This reality is a harbinger of Romans 8:14-17:

> "For all those led by God's Spirit are God's sons. For you did not receive a spirit of slavery to fall back into fear. Instead, you received the Spirit of adoption, by whom we cry out, 'Abba Father!' The Spirit himself testifies together with our spirit that we are God's children, and if children, also heirs—heirs of God and coheirs with Christ—if indeed we suffer with him so that we may also be glorified with him."

There is Trinitarian presence in this transaction.
1. God the Father—"we cry out 'Abba, Father!'" (v. 15).
2. God the Son—"and coheirs with Christ" (v. 17).
3. God the Holy Spirit—"you received the Spirit of adoption" (vs 15).

As believers, we are given an inheritance in Christ.

God's people do not always obey Him. The Israelites' disobedience led to their becoming slaves to another who is not God Almighty. After spending four hundred years in Egyptian bondage, the Exodus occurred. Israel repeated its pattern of sin. The nation spent approximately forty years wandering in the wilderness because they disobeyed God at Kadesh-barnea. **God did not abandon His people. He promised them a new home.**

God is faithful in keeping His promises and is not slack concerning them. God is not in time: time is in God. God's clock keeps perfect providential time. Therefore, God owns time and when He fulfills His promises, they are always fulfilled on time. He is faithful to fulfill His promises.

Eventually, Joshua would inherit a new home, Canaan, which Yahweh promised more than five hundred years earlier to Abraham and his descendants (Genesis 15:18). Yahweh identified the boundaries of the land—north, south, east, and west—even before Moses was born (Genesis 15:18-21). Joshua was the leader who took the people over into the land. This is the omniscience (all-knowingness) of God: knowing the boundaries of the land that was to be possessed even before Joshua and Israel possessed it.

As God's chosen leader, the Spirit rested on Joshua. This was the way the Spirit led, moved, and acted on Old Testament followers of Yahweh. The Spirit would come on Old Testament believers to enable them to accomplish their God-given tasks. Once the tasks were accomplished, then the Spirit would depart from them. This was the case for Samson, one of the mighty judges who led Israel following the death of Joshua. The book of Judges notes that after his head was shaved, Samson did not know that the Lord (Spirit) had departed from him (Judges 16:20). David did not want the Spirit to depart from him either (Psalm 51:11).

The heroes of the Old Testament point beyond themselves to someone greater than themselves. The Old Testament Joshua could only lead the nation of Israel to a land in which they would have to expel and evict the current residents in order to possess the territory. However, Jesus—the greater Joshua—has gone away to prepare a place for believers so that, when they arrive, the only thing that will be necessary is to worship the Triune God, for any hindering causes and people will be dismissed. **He will make all things new in our new home.**

The greater Joshua, Jesus, was conceived by the Spirit, filled with the Spirit without measure, and raised from death by the Spirit (Romans 8:11). After His ascension, the greater Joshua sent the Spirit on the day of Pentecost not to rest on believers but to reside in believers and refill them for effective service (Ephesians 5:18). This is an ongoing process and reality for all believers.

I'm grateful for the book of Joshua and for its treasures. In it lies the precious gem of the gospel: Jesus, the Pearl of great price. He is greater than the Old Testament Joshua in deliverance. He is the deliverer from the bondage of sin and holds the title deed to the heavenly kingdom.

Joshua is replete with the importance of the ark of the covenant as the symbol of God's presence with His people, Israel. At the end of the Bible, in Revelation 21:3, God is not symbolized by an ark composed of Acacia wood. He is actively present in the middle of His people—not in a box but in His own person.

As believers, we are a royal priesthood (1 Peter 2:9). We are sealed by the Spirit until the day of redemption. We are washed in the blood of the crucified One. **We are the children of the Most High God, and we are co-heirs with the greater Joshua, who is the second person of the Trinity.**

The book of Joshua is the written testimony that points to Jesus who not only spoke the Word of God but who is the Word of God. The spoken word of the Old Testament Joshua applied to those who would live in a land of significance, for the land would be the earthly place where the greater Joshua would be born: in the city of Bethlehem of Judea (Micah 5:2) as the revealed word in the incarnation (John 1:14).

Jesus will actually be present with His people in His glorified body with radiance that outshines the sun and glory, that cannot be captured with the pen of the most astute and eloquent writers. God Himself will be among His people.

The God before whom angels bow. The God heaven and earth adore. The God who speaks and it is done; who wills and it comes to pass. The God who cannot be described and yet the God who can be engaged. The God who would not permit Moses to see His glory (Exodus 33:20) but now is on display for all the saints to behold. John says, "They will see his face" (Revelation 22:4) and live in His presence.

And Israel desperately needed His presence. Israel's population during Joshua's leadership was probably over one million. Israel did not have sufficient military strength to defeat the seven nations of Canaan during the three military campaigns: central, northern, and southern. They emerged victoriously and became the landlords of Canaan because the Lord fought for them. In his closing statement, Joshua told the people of Israel they were victorious because "the LORD your God was fighting for you, as he promised" (Joshua 23:10).

Broadly, the first half of the book (Joshua 1–12) is devoted to the possession of the land through the means of war. What's roughly the second half of the book (Joshua 13–24) relates the distribution of the land to the tribes. However, above all else, the reading of Joshua bears witness to Jesus Christ, the greater Joshua.

The Jordan River
ILLUSTRATOR
PHOTO/G.B. HOWELL

1

FAITHFUL TO REVEAL A NEW BEGINNING

JOSHUA 1

Many Americans have a fascination with George Lucas's *Star Wars*. 1983's *Return of the Jedi* left many fans waiting for a new beginning proposed by a cliffhanger when Darth Vader gave a dying message to Luke Skywalker for Luke's sister, Leia. It would be thirty-two years before a new film finally revealed what happened next. But in the mean time, we were left waiting, wanting to know the details of the new beginning.

The book of Joshua begins with a similar scenario. God delivered a cataclysmic announcement which had a catastrophic impact on the minds and hearts of the Israelites: **"Moses my servant is dead"** (Joshua 1:2). This was like a tsunami sweeping over the psychological and emotional surface of the nation. Moses, the great leader of Israel for the past forty years, was dead. Moses, the great mediator of the chosen people of God, was dead. Moses, through whom God worked miracles on behalf of Israel, was dead. Moses, who delivered and taught the Ten Commandments to the nation, was dead. The undeniable questions—possibly so devastating that some did not dare speak the words—were, "Where do we go from here? What do we do now?"

William Shakespeare, the great English playwright, wrote for the character Jacques in *As You Like It*, "All the world's a stage, and all the men and women merely players."[1] Humans are allowed to stand on the stage, perform our acts, and verbalize our speech. Once our performance is over, the lights are turned off, the curtains are dropped, and we make our exit. For the next scene, lights on the stage come on, the curtain is lifted, and new actors perform their roles and play their parts. The play continues.

---

1. William Shakespeare, "Speech: 'All the World's a Stage,'" Poetry Foundation, accessed February 28, 2024, https://www.poetryfoundation.org/poems/56966/speech-all-the-worlds-a-stage.

Moses played his part on the stage of Israel for forty years. After that, God, who is faithful to reveal our new beginnings, told His people their leader had died. Moses exited the stage in the presence of God alone (Deuteronomy 34:1-7). There was not another human leader to tell the story, to alert Israel that it was time to proceed without their leader or to give details of their new beginning. This is God's role, and He is faithful to do His part. God buries His workers, like Moses, but never His work.

God offers three main categories of instruction in Joshua 1: chronography, geography, and autobiography.

Chronography

The word that follows "dead" in Joshua 1:2 is *now*. "Now" suggests immediacy. Deuteronomy 34:8 states that the Israelites mourned the death of Moses for thirty days. God said *now* it is time to move on and cross the Jordan River to claim the land inheritance God promised Abraham over five hundred years earlier.

There is a time for mourning—mourning is real and needed. But there is also a time for moving. After the death of a loved one, the death of a relationship, the death of a dream, or the death of a hope, it is natural and necessary to mourn. But God wants to turn our *mourning* into *morning*. The difference in the spelling of these words is the presence or absence of the letter *u*. Conditions and contexts may not change, but **God can change you so that you can successfully and triumphantly handle the unchanging situations and contexts.**

God told Joshua *now* is the time to move from the east side, the wilderness of Palestine, across the Jordan River to the west side of Canaan, the land flowing with milk and honey. God would fulfill His five-hundred-year-old promise, but to receive the promise, Israel would need to participate in possessing it.

Joshua was the new Moses, and yet he was uniquely Joshua. After the transference of leadership, Joshua had to take the reins handed to and crafted for him by the God of all creation and confidently lead the Israelites into the promised land. God admonished Joshua to fearlessly lead in accordance to what he had seen and heard (Joshua 1:6-7,9).

God gave Joshua trinitarian instructions in verses 6-7 and 9. He told Joshua to be strong and very courageous three times. When God says something once, you know it is important. When He says it twice, you know it is *really* important. Put yourself in Joshua's shoes and imagine how Joshua felt hearing these instructions from God Almighty a third time. Perhaps you have faced the frustration of a parent who has had to repeat instructions more than once. When this happened in my family, my father's voice seemed to change. We knew to obey quickly if he had to repeat the instruction a third time. God ensured Joshua knew to be strong and courageous.

Why would God tell Joshua to be strong and courageous three times? Perhaps God was really telling Joshua to remember his strength came from God. Maybe Joshua did not have natural strength or inherited strength. Maybe he had a measure of strength, but God knew he would need much more to complete his assignment to lead the people of Israel. God gave Joshua what he needed because God is faithful to reveal a new beginning. With this trinitarian instruction, God promised to be with Joshua as He was with Moses.

God was faithful to be with Joshua, as He said. The presence of the Lord was with Moses at the burning bush just as His presence would be with Joshua outside of the city of Jericho. Both Moses and Joshua heard the same divine imperative to take off their shoes for they were standing on holy ground (Exodus 3:5; Joshua 5:15). Joshua had to trust that the same God who led Moses would lead him as he stood before the leaders of the people and delivered the word of the Lord. One day, believers will see our Lord face-to-face (1 John 3:2). We must be strong and know He will fight for us.

Note God's repeated references to time in Joshua 1:2-3, "I *am* giving" and "I *have* given." God gave His gift before it was time to receive it, thereby making His gift a candidate reference from eternity (Ephesians 1:3-6). This is true with our salvation. God declares from eternity that we are adopted, elected, and predestined even before we are born. However, God demonstrates the truth of these pre-existent realities when He brings these about in our lifetime. We come to Christ and receive salvation. **For Joshua and the Israelites, God used time to set the proverbial sure foundation of His faithfulness—faithfulness the Israelites would need to remember since their entire world had been shaken.**

The people said that they had obeyed Moses in all things (Joshua 1:17), but they had not. When Moses stayed at the invitation-only mountaintop conference for longer than the people thought a conference should last, the Israelites had Aaron craft a golden calf that they worshiped as their god (Exodus 32:19). Aaron's apparent fear of the people caused him to lead the people into a great sin against Yahweh in spite of Moses's teaching and in spite of all the things they had witnessed from the hand of God.

Now, Joshua had to lead this short-sighted people into the promised land and corral them to stay together until they conquered the land as they had promised Moses. God's leaders must not rely on the people of God for victory. Like Moses and Joshua, God's leaders must trust and look to the Author and Finisher of their faith for direction and protection that leads to eternal rest. Israel would not take the land; God would give it to them as He promised Abraham (Genesis 12:1-3).

A CLOSER LOOK

Meditate on the Word

"This book of instruction must not depart from your mouth; you are to meditate on it day and night so that you may carefully observe everything written in it" (Joshua 1:8a). God instructed Joshua to meditate on the book of the law day and night.

Whenever I go to the Holy Land, I visit the Wailing Wall in Jerusalem. There, observant Jews pray vocally and utter complete passages of Scripture without reading from the Torah. The Word of the Torah emerges from their hearts as they rock back and forth at the Wailing Wall. With their actions, they are reinforcing the Word that is internalized and is yet being internalized, the Word on which they meditate day and night.

The first two verses of the very first psalm read, "How happy is the one who does not walk in the advice of the wicked or stand in the pathway with sinners or sit in the company of mockers! Instead, his delight is in the LORD's instruction, and he meditates on it day and night." Meditate. The image of meditation carries us to the farm where the cow chews its cud, spits it out, and then chews it again to benefit fully from its nutrients. This is meditation, and it leads to our being "happy" or "blessed," as some translations say. As believers, we are to meditate on the Word of God until Psalm 119:11 becomes our reality. We read it, ingest it, read it again, sing it, and memorize it until we can truthfully say, "I have treasured your word in my heart, so that I may not sin against you."

Promised Geography

In verses 3-4, God delineated the geographical boundaries for the territory Israel would possess in the promised land. This is the same geographical territory that God announced to Abraham in Genesis 15:18-21. **These promises indicate the omnipotence (all powerfulness) and omniscience (all knowingness) of El Shaddai (God Almighty).** It expresses both what Isaiah meant in 46:10 when he said God knows the end before the beginning begins and God's ownership expressed in Genesis 1:1, which says, "In the beginning God created the heavens and the earth."

God gave Israel an area enclosed by four sides—east, west, north, and south: "Your territory will be from the wilderness and Lebanon to the great river, the Euphrates River—all the land of the Hittites—and west to the Mediterranean Sea" (Joshua 1:4). With his announcement, God was faithful to reveal Israel's new beginning and required his children to be faithful in conquering *all* of the territory. Success then and now requires divine-human instrumentality. God's people rely on God and realize victory can only come through their complete obedience to God *wherever their feet shall tread*. Unlike the regional gods worshiped by pagans contemporary to the Israelites who followed Joshua, Yaweh is not bound by land borders, water crossings, air, or depth. As the pagan worshipers would soon learn, Israel's God is El Shaddai everywhere!

In verse 5, the Lord informed Joshua, "No one will be able to stand against you as long as you live." No one. No enemy. No nation. The Israel God chose Joshua to lead would be unconquerable, undefeated, and perpetually victorious. That is, they would be undefeated in battle if they obeyed God. Obedience would allow them to possess their promised possessions.

Yes, the land of promise was something they inherited, but it was not something they were entitled to receive through their own efforts. God does not oppose effort or industry to attain His promises; God opposes earning His promises. We do not earn anything from God, even though we must participate in possessing what He has declared as ours. Believers often pray the portion of Jabez's prayer that highlights the phrase, "Extend my border" (1 Chronicles 4:10). **However, like Israel, we often fail to maximize the use of territories we already possess for God's glory.** Thankfully, our lack of faithfulness does not diminish God's faithfulness. There is no shadow of turning with Him (James 1:17-18).

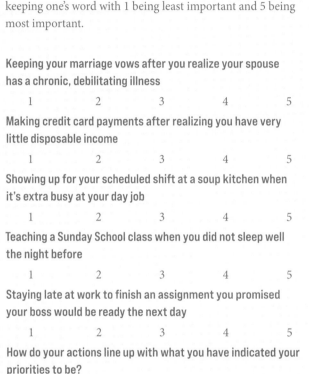

My Word, My Bond

The tribes of Reuben, Gad and half tribe of Manasseh illustrate the importance of keeping our word. Consider the following situations and assign each with a score on the importance of keeping one's word with 1 being least important and 5 being most important.

Keeping your marriage vows after you realize your spouse has a chronic, debilitating illness

   1   2   3   4   5

Making credit card payments after realizing you have very little disposable income

   1   2   3   4   5

Showing up for your scheduled shift at a soup kitchen when it's extra busy at your day job

   1   2   3   4   5

Teaching a Sunday School class when you did not sleep well the night before

   1   2   3   4   5

Staying late at work to finish an assignment you promised your boss would be ready the next day

   1   2   3   4   5

How do your actions line up with what you have indicated your priorities to be?

Canaan is not heaven, but it is a picture of the reality of spiritual warfare in which we continually fight together against the powers of darkness until we reach our heavenly home. The two and a half tribes would leave their families and homes and fight with the nine and a half tribes until they all gained control in the promised land. Similarly, believers must establish Christ's kingdom as priority (Luke 9:57-62). The tribes were so committed, they declared anyone who disobeyed Joshua's imperatives would "be put to death" (Joshua 1:18). The wages of sin is still death (Romans 6:23), but the free gift of God is eternal life through Jesus Christ our Lord who took off His robe of glory to come and conquer sin on behalf of us, His inherited brothers and sisters. We must be unified in our commitment to the kingdom of God.

Believers must develop and maximize our gifts for the glory of God and the edification of others. These opportunities to participate in God's divine order require absolute obedience. God told the Israelites to completely inhabit and control the land He had given them. We will see in Joshua 15:63, 16:10, and 17:12 that the Israelites did not completely evict the Canaanite residents in some of the territories. Their failure would impact their occupation of the promised land.

Autobiography

God chose Joshua as Moses's successor. In so doing, He gave Joshua the opportunity to write his own story. As we saw in Joshua 1:6-7, 9, there is a triple refrain to **"Be strong and courageous."** Why does God have to say the same thing repeatedly to Israel and to us? Are we hard of hearing or do we get convenient amnesia? Parents often ask their children the same question: "How many times am I going to have to tell you?" Those who pastor churches often wonder why their church members don't get the truths of their messages—the same truths they say over and over.

The Hebrew word for teaching carries with it the idea of repetition or redundancy. This divine redundancy is found in Deuteronomy 6, as well. Fathers are told to keep on teaching their children when they sit in their house and when they walk along the road, when they lie down, and when they get up (v. 7). Even the last words of Jesus deal with this redemptive repetition. Jesus says to **teach new disciples "to observe everything I have commanded you"** (Matthew 28:20).

God repeatedly encouraged Joshua to be strong. Why? **Perhaps God reiterated the direction because Joshua was not innately strong. In fact, none of us are innately strong.** We must admit our weaknesses to God, realizing our strength can be found in Him alone. As Paul wrote, believers must constantly confess our weakness to God and ask Him to make us strong (2 Corinthians 12:9-10).

God said to Joshua, **"Be courageous."** This instruction is an imperative, not a suggestive option. **To be courageous, believers recognize their own fear and ineptitude and find boldness in God alone.** Joshua would face foes who were stronger militarily than his military and who had more fighters than Israel. Joshua had an opportunity to agree with God and write his own autobiography of faithful obedience as he walked with God to lead Israel, whose very name means, "God fights!" Like Joshua, we are commanded to be strong and courageous in the face of opposition to God's ways. Joshua was not to turn to the left or the right; he was to keep a straight direction with no deviation from God's revealed path. This is the way we as believers must write our own stories of following our faithful God who fights on our behalf. We write our story by following in His steps and according to His directions with no deviation. We trust God to reveal our new beginnings each time there is an ending.

Altered Biography

Verses 10-18 recount a previous decision. When Moses led Israel, the two and a half tribes of Reuben, Gad, and Manasseh brazenly proposed to alter the cartography of Israel's inheritance. Granting their petition required Moses to have great faith in the tribes' ability to keep their promise—the contemporary equivalent of believing *their word is their bond*. This would change Israel's promised story and offer an altered biography.

As a young boy, my elders often used the phrase, "My word is my bond," and taught us its importance. I lived on a third-floor apartment with my parents and siblings. My mother often sent me to the store to get cold cuts, cheese, bread, milk, juice, or some other staple. However, she did not send me with any money, credit cards, or even a check. She only sent me with her word. I would tell Miss Ann, the store manager, to put the charges on Mama's bill. Miss Ann knew, and I learned, my mother would pay the bill at the end of the month because my Mama's **word was her bond**.

In Numbers 32, the two and a half tribes of Reuben, Gad, and Manasseh found that living on the east side of the Jordan afforded them lush and fruitful territory. They liked it so much, they advocated to have the land as their permanent home. They met with Moses and requested ownership of those conquered territories. These tribes were forfeiting their portion of the unified land with the other nine and a half tribes on the west side of the Jordan. They were changing the story as it had been proposed. They were vacating their promised inheritance. Of course, their request was met with resistance and even anger from Moses, who had risked his life repeatedly to lead Israel to the promised land.

Imagine Moses's disdain for the words attacking his ears and the mistrust burning inside him toward those standing before him. Incomplete understanding can lead to such feelings.

However, the leaders of the two and a half tribes clarified their position. They were not attempting to abandon their responsibility to fight with their relatives to possess the promised land. They simply wanted to leave their families on the east side while they fought to possess what God had already promised. They were altering Israel's biography. Joshua now had to confirm what Moses understood and eventually granted. As the new leader, Joshua would honor the arrangement as long as the two and a half tribes kept their word. They assured Joshua at the risk of death (1:18)—**their word would be their bond**. He only had to be strong and courageous.

Courage in So Many Words

God's people often have to dig down—or look up—to find the courage they need in challenging circumstances. Review these passages below in context to identify just some of the Bible characters and the circumstances they faced when they received a divine message of encouragement.

Genesis 15:1

1 Chronicles 28:20

2 Chronicles 32:7-8

Matthew 14:27

Luke 1:30

Acts 23:11

How might the encouragement they received apply to your life?

A CLOSER LOOK

Stay Focused

Luke 10:38-42 recounts Martha in the kitchen, preparing a meal for Jesus and His followers. Her sister, Mary, was sitting in the parlor at Jesus's feet, listening to His every word.

Martha became agitated with her sister, whom she saw as exemplifying laziness while Martha was sweating in the kitchen. Martha asked Jesus to tell Mary to help her in the kitchen.

Jesus responded, "Martha, Martha, you are worried and upset about many things, but one thing is necessary. Mary has made the right choice, and it will not be taken away from her" (vv. 41b-42). Jesus was saying to Martha, "You are troubled about many things but are missing the main thing." Martha embodies an image of contortion. She was twisted, tied, knotted, and upset about working fretfully to meet physical needs. She was not focused on Jesus who said only one thing was necessary. One thing. Similarly, in Joshua 1, the Lord was saying to Joshua, "Stay focused. Don't turn to the left or to the right. One thing is necessary: follow My lead and My direction so that you and the people you are leading may be prosperous." This is not simply prosperity from a material, physical, or monetary perspective. Following God and focusing on the main thing leads to holistic prosperity—peace of mind, rest of spirit, and tranquility of emotion.

Application Questions

1. Describe a life event that changed the projection of your plans. How did you feel about the change? What steps did you take to understand God's new direction for your life?

2. How have you remained faithful to promises you received from God but have not realized? Which Scriptures help you remember God's faithfulness to reveal your new beginning even in the throes of painful endings?

3. Israel means, "God fights." Romans 8:31 reads, "What, then, are we to say about these things? If God is for us, who is against us?" How does it bolster your faith to know that God fights on behalf of His children?

2

FAITHFUL TO REDEEM

JOSHUA 2

In Joshua 2:1-24, we see God amazingly use defective tools to accomplish His purpose. The defective tools, humans made in God's image, are useful as willing pottery in the hands of the Master Creator who is faithful to redeem. A popular leadership quote proclaims, "Success is not final, failure is not fatal. It is the courage to continue that counts." Rahab epitomized this statement with her life. Her success is intimated by her inclusion in the hall of faith. Hebrews 11:31 says, "By faith Rahab the prostitute welcomed the spies in peace and didn't perish with those who disobeyed." She is acknowledged by James in 2:25 as a prostitute who demonstrated her faith through her works. These are significant attributions since she is identified as a prostitute in Joshua 2:1 as well as 6:17, 22, 25. The former prostitute exhibited great faith by believing God would fight for His people. She employed great works through her faith by saving the spies and, thereby, her own family and became a great grandmother of Jesus through her marriage to a son of Israel, whose people she helped defeat Jericho. She was the wife of Salmon and the mother of Boaz (Matthew 1:5). God is faithful to redeem His own and uses unlikely tools, even fallen humans, to accomplish His purpose.

In his book, *Strength to Love*, Dr. Martin Luther King, Jr. asserted that a person's character could be measured by the depths from which they have emerged.[1] Rahab had a tragic beginning as a prostitute but concluded with a triumphant ending in the biblical hall of faith. But King Saul of the Old Testament had a triumphant beginning but a tragic ending. He began as a son of promise, but he ended on the edge of his own sword (1 Samuel 31:4). Saul was head and shoulders above everybody else (1 Samuel 10:23). He was physically attractive. He was tall. He was respected. The Spirit of God was on him. He even prophesied. Yet as his story unfolds, we watch Saul's downward spiral. God pulled the kingdom away from him, and he had fits

---

1. Martin Luther King, Jr., *Strength to Love* (New York: Beacon Press, 1963).

of melancholy and probably some mental disturbance. He became jealous of David and tried to kill him. He tried to kill Jonathan, his own son. He went to the witch of Endor because the prophet Samuel was dead, and God wouldn't speak to him. Finally, he died on his sword.

By contrast, Saul of the New Testament started off tragically, persecuting the church, and ended having written much of the New Testament. Saul tried to destroy the church by jailing believers and aiding and abetting those who assassinate them (Acts 8:1,3). In the beginning, believers feared him, but in the end, he was a believer who had fought a good fight and kept the faith. He finished his course and was ready to be offered up for this crown of righteous awaiting him (2 Timothy 4:7-8). Though he died a martyr's death, **Saul's life testifies of God's faithfulness to redeem and love Israel through unlikely sources.**

John R. W. Stott, who was the rector of All Souls Church in London from 1950-1975, impacted the world through his sermons and writings. He is credited with writing the greatly influential Lausanne Covenant and embodied, even to his dying days, the determination to finish well. Even his last years were devoted to writing and teaching God's Word. The apostle Paul finished well. In Acts 20:24, he said, "But I consider my life of no value to myself; my purpose is to finish my course and the ministry I received from the Lord Jesus, to testify to the gospel of God's grace."

In 2 Timothy 4:6–8, he said, "For I am already being poured out as a drink offering, and the time for my departure is close. I have fought the good fight, I have finished the race, I have kept the faith. There is reserved for me the crown of righteousness, which the Lord, the righteous Judge, will give me on that day, and not only to me, but to all those who have loved his appearing."

Reverend John Willis, Sr., one of my associates in the ministry at New Mission Baptist Church in Cincinnati, Ohio, finished well. Before he was converted, he was known in our Madisonville community as the town drunk. God saved him and called him to the gospel ministry. He was then revered by the entire community, for everyone could see that a wonderful change had come over him. My mother, Ozella Smith, finished well. The last words she said to me were, "I'll see you in heaven." How we finish says more about us that how we begin. **One may have a disastrous beginning, like Rahab, but be used by God as an unlikely tool of redemption.**

Flawed but Faithful

Read the passages below and fill in the blank to identify the flaws found in some of the Bible's most famous heroes listed in Hebrews 11, the Bible's Hall of Faith:

Genesis 9:21: Noah's sons found him _____
and _____.

Genesis 20:2-12: Abraham _____ and passed off his wife as his sister to protect himself.

Genesis 27: Jacob connived with his mother Rebekah to _____ his father Isaac's blessing from his brother Esau.

Judges 16: Samson could not resist Delilah and _____ the secret of his _____.

2 Samuel 11: David committed _____ with Bathsheba and then arranged the _____ of her husband.

What does this suggest about God's willingness to use people despite their failures?

What was the predominant quality that led God to choose these people for His work in the world?

Trusted Tools in God's Hands

In Numbers 13:1-2, God instructed His servant Moses to select one person out of each of the twelve tribes and send them as spies to survey the land, inspect the land, and provide a report upon their return. Twelve of them went out, and twelve of them returned. However, ten of the twelve gave a report of despair. They told Moses and the congregation that the Israelites could not defeat the Canaanites because the Canaanites had giants who made the Israelites look like grasshoppers. Therefore, they could not militaristically match the Canaanites. But two trusted servants of God (and unlikely tools), Caleb and Joshua, gave a minority report with major faith. They acknowledged the challenge before them and discussed the fruitfulness of the land.

They noted the giants in the land but also that their God would enable them to fight the battles and be victorious. Caleb and Joshua understood the power of trusted tools in God's redeeming hands. The Israelites rejected the minority report of Caleb and Joshua and accepted the majority report of the other ten spies. This resulted in the children of Israel delaying their going into the promised land for about forty years. Forty years later, Joshua sent spies on a reconnaissance mission—but not twelve this time, only two. They were to go to the fortress city of Jericho, for this was the first city of military combat. The strategy was to divide and conquer.

After they conquered Central Palestine (Jericho), then they would defeat the south and the north. These two spies visited the house of sin in Jericho: Rahab's house of prostitution, an unlikely place for redemption. Light isn't supposed to go into darkness but is to come out of darkness as light. These men were selected and must have been men of integrity. They must have known to flee youthful lusts. They must have been taught to resist the devil so that he would flee. They must have had enough faith to stand.

I'm sure the house of prostitution was the grassroots grapevine of those times, where the news traveled and where information was given. It was also a place where one could ordinarily escape and avoid suspicion. However, these two spies were spotted and reported to the king of Jericho, who sent the JPD (Jericho Police Department) to Rahab's house to inquire about the spies and, undoubtedly, to take them into custody. Before the JPD arrived, Rahab had already hidden the spies on the roof and covered them with flax. When the JPD arrived, Rahab informed them that it was true that the men had come to her but had since left the city. She counseled them to immediately pursue the spies and apprehend them in the mountains. The JPD left the city in search of the men. Of course, this was a lie. God does not condone lying but can recycle a lie and use it to accomplish His purpose—in this case, the sparing of the spies, which enabled them to return to Joshua and give their report. Rahab the prostitute was a trusted servant in the hands of our redeeming God.

We must remember that Abraham, the father of the faithful, lied to Pharaoh regarding his wife. But God still used him, an unlikely tool. Then, we have Joseph, who was known for what happened to him because of others' sins. In Genesis 50:20, Joseph said to his brothers, "You planned evil against me; God planned it for good to bring about the present result—the survival of many people." He was saying that even though his brothers sold him into slavery, God raised him up to become the vice regent in Egypt where he spearheaded the food storage plan that eventually saved his family. Joseph was sold and became an unlikely tool God used to redeem His people. His brothers' ungodly actions ultimately spared Judah, the fourth son of Jacob, through whom Jesus Christ would come.

All of us are sinners and God saved us. Though broken, we must be willing vessels to carry out His redemptive purposes. Paul admonishes in 1 Corinthians 6:9-11, "Don't you know that the unrighteous will not inherit God's kingdom? Do not be deceived: No sexually immoral people, idolaters, adulterers, or males who have sex with males, no thieves, greedy people, drunkards, verbally abusive people, or swindlers will inherit God's kingdom. And some of you used to be like this. But you were washed, you were sanctified, you were justified in the name of the Lord Jesus Christ and by the Spirit of our God."

Unlikely Acts of Redemption

John Newton was converted in 1748, at the age of 23. His first voyage as a slave ship captain was three years later. He did not write a critical word against the slave trade until years after his last voyage in 1754, and did not publicly declare himself against the practice until the 1780s—three decades after his last voyage.[2] John Newton, as a slave ship captain, was an unlikely

---

2. Melissa Petruzzello, "John Newton," Encyclopædia Britannica, February 10, 2024, https://www.britannica.com/biography/John-Newton; John Piper, "John Newton: The Tough Roots of His Habitual Tenderness," Desiring God, January 30, 2001, https://www.desiringgod.org/messages/john-newton-the-tough-roots-of-his-habitual-tenderness.

tool. However, in the hands of our redeeming God, he wrote the great hymn "Amazing Grace," with lyrics many of us identify with: **"Amazing grace, how sweet the sound that saved a wretch like me."**

When we see ourselves through the lens of the Creator, we realize our need to be patient with unlikely tools like Rahab. Yes, according to James 2:25, she is justified; however, **sanctification is progressive development and conformity to the will and the way of God.** We can rejoice because we are works in progress, and God is not finished with us yet. He's refining us like gold and will one day complete the work He began in us (Philippians 1:6). **God uses defective tools to accomplish His purpose.**

Rahab testified that they had heard of how God had fought for His people in Israel's defeat of the Amorite kings and also of how God had parted the Red Sea so that the children of Israel could cross on dry ground. Notice she said she had heard. This anticipates how faith is born, as Paul says in Romans 10:17, "So faith comes from what is heard, and what is heard comes through the message about Christ." Rahab admitted that the hearts of the Jerichoites were melting—that is, they were panicking. She acknowledged that Israel would win. Even though the city of Jericho had massive walls, she testified Israel would win because God was fighting for them (Joshua 23:3,10). Rahab was establishing in her testimony that God is sovereign both in heaven and in earth and that willing people, just and unjust, could be used by Him.

As Christians, we are more than conquerors through Christ who loves us. The war is already over, and Satan has already lost. But the enemy is continuing his ongoing battle with the children of God. Satan is fronting: He already knows he is defeated. Christians only need to recognize this fact to begin engaging Satan *from* victory to victory and not trying to fight *for* victory. The victory is already ours—unlikely tools in the hands of a redeeming God!

Unlikely Redemptive Reversal

After the JPD left to pursue the two spies, Rahab went up to the roof, uncovered the spies, and began to bargain. Apparently, she was a good bargainer. She had formerly bargained for funds from her customers, and now she bargained to save the lives of her family members. It's "Let's Make a Deal" time for her. It's "I scratched your back, now it's time for you to scratch mine." It's an unlikely redemptive reversal where the unsaved saves then asks the saved to save her and others. She asked the two spies to make an oath in the name of God that when the Israelites attacked Jericho, her family would be spared. **The spies made a covenant with her.** They essentially said, "When we come to attack this city, this crimson cord must be placed outside your window as a way of identifying this unlikely divine protective custody order for members of your family. Any family member that is not in your house will not be covered and will not be spared. Those who are in your house will be safeguarded."

This is reminiscent of the ark during the flood. Only those who were in the ark during the flood were spared, and that included just eight people: Noah, his wife, his three sons, and their wives. No one outside of the ark would be spared. This is also reminiscent of the first Passover. The homes smeared with the blood of Passover lambs were spared. The death angel would come by at a divinely appointed time and pass over the houses with the door posts and lintels smeared with blood. Households that were not identified by the blood experienced the death of their firstborn son.

Rahab became an evangelist to her own family. She took advantage of the time because she did not know exactly when Joshua and the Israelites would attack the city. Just as Noah attempted to tell the people of his generation to come into the ark, Rahab realized the urgency of their situation and told her family to come into the house.

Let's consider a rational countdown. The spies left Jericho and stayed in the mountains for three days before crossing over the fords of the Jordan and returning to Joshua. They spent one day consecrating themselves before they crossed the Jordan. They spend one or more days crossing the Jordan, since there were more than a million people. Seven days expired as they recovered from circumcision. Seven days passed as they walked in procession around the walls of Jericho. That gave Rahab about three weeks to knock on her relatives' doors, telling them to come into the house of redemption.

When we consider our unsaved relatives and friends, we should have this same urgency. Rahab was taking a real risk because she knew that if it was revealed to the JPD and the king of Jericho that she was collaborating with the Israelite spies, she would undoubtedly be killed. But she also knew Joshua and the Israelites were going to completely destroy the city, so she chose to take her chances with God. This is called faith. In our society, dangers accompany standing on the truth of Scripture and even mentioning Jesus in certain circles. Thankfully, we can trust the unlikely redemptive reversals that are promised to us if we exercise our faith in God.

A CLOSER LOOK

Meditate on the Word

The apostle Paul wrote, "For I consider that the sufferings of this present time are not worth comparing with the glory that is going to be revealed to us" (Romans 8:18). He boldly lived his theology of suffering while fixing his eyes firmly on God's promise of life everlasting through Jesus Christ. Paul proclaimed his ability to finish his course well although he had been beaten, rejected, shipwrecked, and confronted and chastised on the Damascus road by the Christ. Some might consider his life a failure since he poured himself out for Christ after having spent much time fervently persecuting those who followed that same Jesus—which he did with much support from the political and religious elite.

The sixteenth-century reformer Martin Luther criticized the Scholastics because they majored in and emphasized the theology of achievement and attainment and underemphasized the theology of suffering. Luther believed these theological orders needed to be reversed to retain the redemptive rhythm and sanctified sequence, thus aligning with biblical theology. In Luther's thought, the theology of the cross (suffering) always preceded the theology of glory.

Jesus told His disciples they would face persecution in the world but to take courage because He had *conquered* the world (John 16:33). As believers weigh our pursuit of life, liberty, and happiness, Scripture calls us to consider our theology of suffering and its impact on our evangelism. Like Rahab, we are challenged to choose what to believe and determine how that belief is demonstrated in our daily life, witness, and discipleship.

Jericho's Biblical Storied History

The battle for Jericho and the fall of its walls may be the most famous event, which puts the city on a historical map. But Jericho was also the site of other fascinating vignettes during Bible times. We know the place, but do we know its significance in the New Testament? Read the passages below to identify the main characters and what happened to them there.

Analyze the passage as a critical thinker to identify the theme.

	CHARACTER(S)	PLOT	THEME
Matthew 20:29-34			
Luke 10:25-37			
Luke 19:1-10			

Unlikely Escape through Unlikely Tools

In Joshua 2:7, the gates were shut so that there would be no entrance into or exit from the city. Yet the two spies were able to leave the city. How? They were let out through a window. When doors are closed, God opens windows. No wonder Malachi 3:10 says that God will open the windows of heaven and Revelation 3:8 says that God opens doors that no one can shut. God specializes in things that seem impossible, and He can use unlikely tools to redeem His own.

Darryl Strawberry, a former Major League Baseball player, tremendously hindered and undoubtedly shortened his baseball career through his use of alcohol and drugs. After his career ended, he yielded to God and started preaching the gospel. He now has a thriving ministry, and his motto is, "Make your mess your message."[3] This is what happened to Rahab: she made her mess her message. Throughout Scripture, God calls people to make their mess their message. The Samaritan woman who had a suspicious reputation and a checkered past had an encounter with Jesus, and then she went to her hometown and told the men to come see a man who told her everything she had done. "Is this not the Christ?" she asked. She made her mess her message.

These two spies carried out the instructions of Rahab, who told them to escape Jericho, go into the mountains, and stay there for three days before returning to the Israelite camp. When they reported their unlikely story of redemption to Joshua, they rejoiced because Jericho was on God's docket for destruction. God had already given them the victory. God had already prepared Joshua to recognize unlikely tools in the hands of a redeeming God.

Fourteen hundred years later, the New Testament Joshua, Jesus, went to Jericho in Luke 19. There, he called the unscrupulous Zacchaeus down from the sycamore tree. Zacchaeus was the director of the Internal Revenue Service at Jericho. He was employed by the Roman government, and as a publican, he stole from his own Jewish people. However, when Jesus went to his house, Zacchaeus was converted and became known as "a son of Abraham" (Luke 19:9).

---

3. Robert Smith Jr., *Exalting Jesus in Joshua*, ed. David Platt, Daniel L. Akin, and Tony Merida, Christ-Centered Exposition Commentary (Brentwood, TN: Holman Reference, 2023), 44.

Eventually, Jesus died in the city of Jerusalem for all of us who are people of sin, like those unlikely persons redeemed in Jericho. God is faithful to redeem and can use defective tools to accomplish His purposes through the blood of His sinless and perfect Son, the Lamb, who redeems us as His own.

A CLOSER LOOK

Stay Focused

In Joshua 2, we are introduced to Rahab the prostitute. Have you considered what drew the spies to Rahab? What qualities might she have possessed and wielded to get the respect of the JPD officers, who followed her instructions without doubting? Perhaps she was beautiful. Perhaps she spoke eloquently and intelligently. Whatever the reason, human eyes and perceptions guided others' perceptions of the worth of her words, regardless of her position. Jesus promised His followers blessings if we have pure hearts (Matthew 5:8). Carefully consider the posture of your heart and the hearts of those you listen to. Amid the noise and the things most valued in your society, stay attuned to the voice of God. Your blessings will follow the posture of your heart.

Application Questions

1. In this lesson, an unlikely servant lied. How can a well-intentioned person who lies be used for God's redemptive purposes? How can grace for sinful actions be seen as an act of a just and perfect God?

2. Consider major events in your life. With which character mentioned in this lesson do you most identify? How does that identification encourage you as an unlikely tool in the hands of our redeeming God?

3. How does the juxtaposition of worldly wisdom compare and contrast with the foolishness of obeying God? For example, it is often believed that the majority rules, but Caleb and Joshua's minority report was actually God's report. How would you help an unbeliever choose God's way?

3

FAITHFUL TO LEAD

JOSHUA 3–4

The Jordan crossing, like so many other miraculous biblical events, reminds us that God is living and active in our world. He did not write the story of time, wind the clock of destiny, and stand back to watch things unfurl. He cares about His creation. The old adage "better late than never" could apply to the Israelite community of over one million people crossing the Jordan River in Joshua 3–4. It should have taken a few weeks because it was "an eleven-day journey from Horeb to Kadesh-barnea" (Deuteronomy 1:2), the desert of wandering.

God has shown His faithfulness to lead throughout Israel's history. One can argue leadership is an innate need. When I was a boy, we would play games like follow-the-leader and red light, green light. Each game required the players to watch a leader closely to win.

Leaders are good for followers. God demonstrated this truth when He gave instructions to Adam and Eve. Today's society has many pundits who define leaders by the characteristics of those who follow. However, the Bible demonstrates a follower's unwillingness to follow does not diminish the leader's faithfulness, effectiveness, or call to lead.

I vividly remember one Christmas when my children were young. I had purchased a bicycle for my oldest son, Bobby. It was the night before Christmas, and all through the night, I took the bicycle parts out of the box. It was such a sight! Anyone who knows me knows I am not good with my hands, but I was determined to try.

I began to assemble the bike, and I thought I was making progress until I noticed a problem after installing the handlebars: they were backward. As I continued, things only got worse. That was when I finally had a brilliant revelation: read the manufacturer's instructions! When I read the instructions, I immediately knew I had to disassemble what I had done and start over.

After several hours, I finally got it right and had a bicycle to present to my son on Christmas Day. Before my revelation, some facts were evident: I had the bike and, without a doubt, Christmas was coming. I just needed to realize the importance of following the instructions provided for me to assemble a bike that would function according to the manufacturer's promise.

Similarly, the Israelites had God's promise, and the day of reckoning was approaching. He was their ultimate leader who was faithful to lead. They had to take the territory and could not rely on their own ingenuity or plans. They had been unfaithful followers before, but they would need to carefully follow the instructions of the Lord to reach the promised land.

Leaders Lead while Followers Choose

God's leadership protocol is evident in the book of Joshua. Instructions flowed from God to Joshua, from Joshua to the elders, and from the elders to the people. At every stage, the instructions needed to be faithfully received, faithfully delivered, and faithfully followed.

At the time of the text, Israel stood at the edge of the Jordan River, ready to cross over into the promised land. As we know, it was an eleven-day journey from the Mount Sinai/Horeb range to Kadesh-barnea. Kadesh-barnea was 177 miles (285.7 kilometers) from the Jordan River—that's approximately the distance from New York City to Boston, Massachusetts (190 miles). In a car today, it would take a little less than three hours to drive from Boston to NYC. To walk from Kadesh-barnea to the Jordan River with over one million people consisting of pregnant women, seniors, infants, youth, and young and middle-aged adults would have taken a few weeks . . . that is, if the Israelites had not hesitated and balked at Kadesh-barnea. **They traded in a few weeks' journey and settled for nearly four decades of wandering in the wilderness.**

The great regrets of the saints and sages through the ages are missed opportunities and wasted time during their earthly pilgrimage. As they reflect, believers see they could have accomplished more for the kingdom had they allowed the Lord to order their steps and their stops. Too often, we believers step when the Lord says stop and run ahead of God like Abram did in the Hagar narrative. He did not wait for God to fulfill His promise of a son through Abram's aged wife Sarai. Other times, believers lag behind God and miss the Lord's appointed moment, like at Kadesh-barnea. Israel had come to an important point: it was time to cross the Jordan River.

To prepare the Israelites, God instructed Joshua and the people to remain before the Jordan River for three days. After three days and receiving instruction from the officers, the Israelites would be ready to cross into the promised land.

They would be guided by God's word and empowered by His Spirit. Spirit and Word cannot be separated. Too many churches take pride in being "Word churches," but they reject the Spirit. Other churches boast about being "Spirit churches" but are unwilling to be informed and led by the Word of God. A church that is a so-called "Spirit church," absent of the Word, is a church of inspiration without information; a church that boasts about being a "Word church" and rejects the Spirit is a church of information without inspiration. We need both the Word and the Spirit. God cannot be trichotomized: He is a trinitarian God and never acts outside of His trinitarian nature.

The people were instructed to keep their eyes on the ark of the covenant that would be carried by the Levitical priests. They would remain in place until the priests moved with the ark. If the priests with the ark did not move, the Israelites were not to move. They would faithfully follow the ark while remaining about a thousand yards behind it so they could clearly see its direction, follow its movement, and show reverence for God. The separation was also for safety. Numbers 4 instructed the Israelites to take staves or poles and insert them through rings on either side of the ark so that the ark could be carried on the priests' shoulders without the priests coming in contact with the ark. The ark represented deity—God—and the priests, as well as the entire congregation, represented dust.

This ark would be their spiritual GPS and inherent protector. No matter how intuitive they thought their travels would be, they had not passed that way before. No matter how skilled they were at following tracks or noting changes in the wind, they would need to trust the One who would faithfully lead them well. So, the people consecrated themselves for the great wonders the Lord would do on the next day.

The ark of the covenant was a wooden box of acacia wood that was overlaid by gold; in fact, gold lined the inside of the box, as well as covered its lid (Exodus 25:11). On either end rested two angelic beings known as cherubim, hammered out of gold, that faced each other and lifted up their wings toward heaven in a posture of worshiping God (Exodus 25:18-20).

The contents within the ark of the covenant were very important. They represented historical memorabilia to remind the children of Israel of what God had done among them. First, there was a copy of the

Ten Commandments, which represented the **proclamation** of the Word of God. There was also a pot of manna, which symbolized God's **provision**. Finally, there was Aaron's rod that budded almonds, which served as a sign of God's power (Hebrews 9:4).

During their nearly forty-year wilderness journey, God had given them His Word in the form of the Ten Commandments. The Ten Commandments provided six prohibitions—things that they were prohibited from doing— and four exhortations—four admonitions that they were to observe. **This was God's proclamation.**

During their journey in the wilderness, God sent bread from heaven six days a week for forty years so the Israelites would survive the arduous journey. Some considered it angels' food. They were to gather it for six days a week and to gather twice as much on the sixth day to cover them for the seventh day when no manna would fall. **This was God's provision.**

Aaron's rod was just a regular wooden stick that produced buds, blossoms and eventually almonds without the benefit of soil, water or photosynthesis. Almonds budded from what seemed to be just an old, dry stick. This illustrated God's **power.**

How could they fail knowing they had God's Word, God's provision and God's power? Of course, we no longer have the ark of the covenant today. Instead, we have something better: Jesus, who perfectly embodies everything the ark contained and to which its contents pointed.

The Lord had already prepared His leader as well. He told Joshua He would be with him in the same way He had been with Moses. God's presence would not only assure Joshua but also confirm Joshua's appointment by God as the leader for God's people. God's presence would let the people know Joshua was chosen by God and not a self-appointed leader or merely a leader selected by Moses to be Moses's replacement.

Then and now, leadership is so important to God that He takes great care to appoint those He has anointed to lead His people. Followers need only look for the genuine presence of God, knowing the Lord is faithful to lead His leaders. God publicly inaugurated and certified Joshua in the sight of all Israel on the next day as a way of exalting His divinely appointed leader (Joshua 3:7). The time had come to move from the wilderness to the land of promise.

Arguably, the Israelites were to cross the Jordan at a time of customary floods. It would be spring, and the frozen waters on Mount Hermon would cause flooding in the plains where the Israelites were poised to cross. These facts should have encouraged and not seemed odd to the Israelites.

God would hold back the water for them at the Jordan River, just like He did at the Red Sea when the waters stood up as the children of Israel crossed over into the wilderness forty years earlier. This promise of God's faithfulness should have installed confidence in the Israelites as, forty years later, God was leading His people out of the wilderness. God had delivered instructions to Joshua; Joshua delivered them to the leaders; and for three days, the leaders delivered them to the people. With their God who was faithful to lead, the Israelites had every reason to believe they would be successful in crossing into and evicting the seven resident nations from the land of Canaan.

A CLOSER LOOK

Consecrate Yourself

In Joshua 3:5, Joshua told the Israelites to, "Consecrate yourselves, because the LORD will do wonders among you tomorrow." God's presence for the wonders He would do required the people to set themselves apart. Strong's Concordance includes *sanctify, prepare, dedicate,* and *separate* as words to define consecrate.[1] The Israelites prepared themselves for what God was going to do among them, even though they would be at least two thousand yards away from God's presence! Consecrating is something believers are called to do today. However we consecrate, we should focus on being cleansed with the Living Water and separating ourselves from sin. As Paul wrote in Colossians 3:8-10, "But now, put away all the following: anger, wrath, malice, slander, and filthy language from your mouth. Do not lie to one another, since you have put off the old self with its practices and have put on the new self. You are being renewed in knowledge according to the image of your Creator." Our partnership in consecration requires believers to trust and follow our faithful Leader.

---

1. James Strong, *A Concise Dictionary of the Words in the Greek Testament and The Hebrew Bible* (Bellingham, WA: Logos Bible Software, 2009), 102.

Consecrate Yourself

Joshua ordered the Israelites to consecrate themselves to prepare for the crossing of the Jordan River and battle of Jericho. His admonition to his people is not the only one of this kind you will find in the Bible.

Read Romans 12:1 to fill in these blanks:

Therefore, brothers and sisters, in view of the _____
of _____, I urge you to present your _____
as a living _____, holy and pleasing to God; this is your
true _____.

List some of the ways you can live up to this verse.

1.

2.

3.

4.

5.

Following in Faith

It was time to begin the procession across the Jordan River. The priests carried the ark. As soon as their feet touched the edge of the Jordan River, God stopped the waters from flowing downstream. The priests carrying the ark stood in the middle of the Jordan River with *dry feet* while the entire Israelite community crossed over into the promised land.

The priests could have stood at the edge of the Jordan River without the ark of the covenant and with their feet touching the water's edge, and the Jordan River would have kept on flowing. The ark of the covenant was what made the difference. **We may preach, sing, and serve in the ministry of the church in many ways, but without the presence of God among us and in our lives, we will not see the proclamation of the Word of God, the provision of God, or the power of God.** We will simply be going through the motions.

God was providing for Joshua and the children of Israel a preview of coming attractions. They knew they would face enemies that seemed formidable and cities that appeared to be indestructible. They knew Canaan was inhabited by seven nations: the Canaanites, Hittites, Hivites, Perizzites, Girgashites, Amorites, and Jebusites. The miracle that took place at the Jordan River was a demonstration that if God could hold back the river until the whole nation had crossed over, then God could defeat this sevenfold nation of Canaan.

Once again, God proved Himself faithful to His people. After the Israelites crossed over, Joshua selected one man from each of the twelve tribes to build an altar. As their newly consecrated leader, he gave specific instructions to take a boulder from where the priests stood with the ark and lay the stones on top of the altar at Gilgal as a rock memorial of remembrance for future generations.

One might wonder why a memorial was necessary. Israel had proven to be a forgetful people. God had done miracles during the days of Miriam and Aaron, yet they questioned God's choice of Moses as leader. God had kept the Israelites through slavery and brought them out of the land of Egypt, yet they yearned to return when the corner store did not have their favorite food.

Leaders must be familiar with their followers. God knew the Israelites needed signs to prompt their memory of divine visitations. Jesus chastised the religious leaders for relying too heavily on signs (Matthew 16:4).

Joshua instructed the people to build a memorial so that when young children of future generations asked what the stones meant, adults could say they signified how God created the blockade at the Jordan River to grant the Israelites safe passage into the promised land.

After the last Israelite crossed over into the promised land, the ark-bearing priests marched into Canaan. Once the priests' feet came out of the Jordan River and touched the dry land of Canaan, the waters resumed their flow. This was not luck. It was not an "abracadabra," "open sesame" form of trickery. This was the sovereign hand of God at work. God is never acting before time or after time: He is always on time. The priests stood in the middle of the Jordan River like school crossing guards until the entire nation had crossed over on dry ground.

The very heartbeat of this passage is the presence of the ark of the covenant, which represents the presence of God among of His people. In fact, the hero of Joshua chapters three and four is God. God is the center of all the activity. God is the foundation, the stabilizing agent, the all-powerful deity, and the faithful leader. Their journey highlighted these truths. When the ark moved, the people moved. Where the ark turned, the people turned. When the ark stopped, the people stopped.

In Joshua, the ark was in the form of a wooden box. In the New Testament, the ark came in the form of a human body: Jesus, whose name shall be called Immanuel, God with us (Matthew 1:23). The apostle John put it this way: "The Word became flesh and dwelt among us. We observed his glory, the glory as the one and only Son from the Father, full of grace and truth" (John 1:14). **As believers, we follow the leader with the indwelling presence of God since the ark also points to the Spirit of God who leads and guides us into all truth (John 16:13).**

However, the Spirit's presence alone does not grant us the ability to proceed through life without error. Just as the Israelites followed the ark and were given instructions by God for crossing over the Jordan River, so believers must obey the Holy Spirit who leads believers to follow God so their greater Joshua is ultimately exalted. We must cultivate a relationship with God. We must pray and trust the Holy Spirit to lead us into all truth. We must take up our cross daily and follow our faithful Leader.

Memorializing Miracles

The ark of the covenant and the stones of the Jordan are just two examples in Joshua of marking the amazing ways God blessed His people or intervened on their behalf. Read each passage below to see how others memorialized God's work in their lives.

Genesis 12:7: _____ built an altar.

Genesis 35:1-14: Jacob built an _____.

1 Chronicles 22: David prepared to build the _____.

Luke 1: 46-55: _____ composed and sang a song after experiencing God's divine revelation.

1 Corinthians 11:17-24: Jesus's followers observed His _____ through a shared meal.

Luke 24:1-6: Generations of Christians celebrate Jesus's _____ at Easter.

List some ways to memorialize God's sacred touch in your life.

A CLOSER LOOK

Stay Focused

The Israelites Joshua led did not have firsthand knowledge of the crossing of the Red Sea. Of course, many of them wandered in the wilderness during the forty-year period incited by their parents' disobedience. God did not allow most of the previous generation to enter the promised land: Caleb and Joshua alone remained from their generation (Numbers 14:29-31). The Israelites would need to know God and His mighty acts for themselves, just as believers are required to make a personal confession of faith. It is tempting to listen only to what others say about God, the Bible, or living a life of faith. Joshua 4 reminds us of the need to know our history and to teach others. Joshua said, "'In the future, when your children ask their fathers, 'What is the meaning of these stones?' you should tell your children, 'Israel crossed the Jordan on dry ground.' For the LORD your God dried up the water of the Jordan before you until you had crossed over, just as the LORD your God did to the Red Sea, which he dried up before us until we had crossed over. This is so that all the peoples of the earth may know that the LORD's hand is strong, and so that you may always fear the LORD your God'" (Joshua 4:21-24). Stay focused, and tell the story.

Application Questions:

1. How can the physical and/or spiritual presence of God help believers learn to obey?

2. Ephesians 1:4-5 says God chose believers to be holy and blameless before Him. How does human will impact God's purposes and plans? Can a people group, like the Israelites, collectively deny God's perfect plan for them? How can their decisions impact others?

3. The Israelites had the history of God opening the Red Sea to help them believe He could lead them across the Jordan River, even at flood stage. What history do you use to encourage yourself about God's faithfulness to lead you on His chosen path for your life?

4

FAITHFUL TO DELIVER

JOSHUA 6

By Joshua 6, the Israelites had consecrated themselves. Circumcision, Passover, and the Feast of Unleavened Bread had been observed. They were now ready to march against the fortress city of Jericho. To understand the power of the text, though, one has to understand Israel as they appear in God's eyes. The name Israel means "God fights," and the Lord would fight for Israel. In essence, God fought the battle of Jericho, and the walls came tumbling down! This is an account of divine/human instrumentality.

This is good news for believers. Isaiah 43:1 assures believers that God has called us by name and claims us as His own. He requires His people to do their part to receive and participate in their deliverance, but He is not slack regarding His promises. God is faithful to deliver. In the battle of Jericho, we see that God fought on behalf of His people. But His people were required to act in obedience to receive their deliverance.

God's Promise to Deliver

Joshua 6 begins with a daunting statement, if human strength alone was expected to win the battle of Jericho: "Now Jericho was strongly fortified because of the Israelites—no one leaving or entering" (Joshua 6:1). Jericho was locked up. However, our God is not bound by human devices. He cannot be locked out or locked in by human or any other means. Revelation 3:7 reminds us only God opens doors that no one can close.

God guaranteed that Jericho would be defeated, saying, "I have given you every place where the sole of your foot treads" (v. 3). However, He did not release Israel from their responsibility to participate in the battle. It was only when Israel possessed their possession that their possession was really theirs (Joshua 1:3-4). We are not permitted to presume on God. We must participate in the dynamic of divine/human instrumentality.

A CLOSER LOOK

Check Your Perception

In Joshua 6:2b, God said, "Look, I have handed Jericho, its king, and its best soldiers over to you." God gave His promise to deliver. In fact, He helped Joshua be courageous by telling him the outcome before the battle began. In His promise to deliver, God started with the command to look. God was not using "look" casually or as a filler word: He instructed Joshua to perceive, to understand, to study, and to know God had given the battle of Jericho to Israel.

Proverbs 3:5-6 instructs believers: "Trust in the LORD with all your heart, and do not rely on your own understanding; in all your ways know him, and he will make your paths straight." The Holy Spirit leads and guides us into all truth (John 16:13-15). As we experience life with our eyes on God, we can trust the Holy Spirit to reveal the things we need to know to live according to God's commands.

Trusting God requires a proper perspective and perception. Just as the Israelites obeyed a strange battle plan, believers must yield and obey God, even when we do not understand His plan (Isaiah 55:8-9). We must study to perceive, to understand, and to know God is sovereign. Our obedience is more important than our limited understanding. Check your perspective.

God's Plan of Deliverance

God started by giving Joshua the battle plan, and it was the most unusual military plan imaginable. The assigned groups are to march around the massive walls of Jericho. Josephus, the intertestamental Jewish historian, estimates that the walls of Jericho were so massive and wide that two chariots could ride on the wall side by side safely.

The military march would be a peculiar procession. It would draw ire and scorn from spectators. Armed soldiers would lead the procession, followed by the priests bearing horns (shofars) that they would blow continuously. Priests carrying the ark of the covenant would follow, then more armed

South of Jericho, Israel, where Joshua and Israel camped before going to Jericho, found near Old Testament Jericho
ILLUSTRATOR PHOTO/G.B. HOWELL

soldiers would comprise the rear guard. These are clear instructions, but they do not sound like a viable battle plan. Though the plan seemed uncustomary, the Israelites would need to meticulously obey God's instructions to receive their deliverance.

The Israelites were to make one complete revolution around the city walls once a day for six days and seven times on the seventh day without the sound of a human voice. At the end of the seventh revolution on the seventh day, the horn would continue sounding, the people would shout, and the walls would come tumbling down. The rest of the Israelites would rush into the city and completely destroy the population of Jericho.

God is in both silence and sound. Too often, in our churches, we discern the presence of God only in sound or noise. We are too uncomfortable with silence. For many believers, when there is the absence of sound and the presence of silence, they simply say the worship is dead. And yet there must be time in the worship service for silent meditation, contemplation, and cogitation. Celebration is important, but so is cogitation. **In fact, the more we cogitate and percolate about the goodness of the Lord and what He has done for us, the more we celebrate.** The more experience we have in solitude and quiet, the stronger we will be when it is time to make a joyful sound. Like David, we love to praise the Lord with stringed instruments and organs and high-sounding cymbals. However, God is also in silence.

Mary, the mother of Jesus, simultaneously and inextricably held silence and sound together. On the one hand, there was great silence after the angel Gabriel informed her she would be the mother of the Son of God. She pondered those things in her heart. This is silence. She meditated and contemplated what the angel said to her. But on the other hand, she expressed sound in her song, which is often called the Magnificat (Luke 1:46-47). Silence and sound are not antithetical; they are commensurate, and at times, both are absolutely necessary.

The blowing of the horns and the ensuing shouting of the people were notes of anticipation even before they saw the sign of victory, namely the collapse of the walls. Surely, it must have produced great ridicule on the part of the people of Jericho when they heard the blowing of the horns as the priests marched around the walls on that seventh day. Nothing victorious had yet occurred. This is a picture of faith. Believers must exercise faith not passively but actively. They must celebrate in anticipation of deliverance. They must celebrate in expectation of recovery. Anyone can celebrate after the walls fall, but can we thank God before they fall, knowing the walls will fall because God said they will?

God instructs this group of people to march around the walls one time each day for six days, and seven times on the seventh day. That's thirteen revolutions, thirteen circuits, thirteen rounds. Why all of this marching? Could not God have brought the walls down after one time around on the first day? Yes! Could it be that God wanted this military regime and these priests to become so acquainted with the massive walls that they would recognize the building components with each successive revolution? The stones in the wall were not at all weakened. The stones were just as intact upon completion of their thirteenth round as they were when they made their first circuit. Could it be He wanted them to know that they were helpless in gaining entrance to Jericho without Him? Could it be that God wanted them to realize, without Him telling them, that if the walls were to fall, He would have to bring them down Himself? We know this is a lesson believers need to learn today: **The power to defeat our Jerichos will not come through our methods, skills, reputations, titles, or any of the things we take pride in doing in order to be victorious.** God will have to do it!

Where was Joshua in the procession? We are not told. He must have been in the procession because he gave the order for the people to shout. Joshua's position as a human leader was significant, but he was not indispensable. The ark of the covenant representing God's presence with His people is indispensable. Joshua conveyed the word of God to the people. As human leaders, we get directions from God and convey them to the people. It is not important that we are seen: it is important that God is seen; it is important that Jesus is glorified; and it is important that the Holy Spirit is present.

Divine/Human Instrumentality for Deliverance

The people in the camp were organized into four groups and instructed not to talk as they marched around the walls until Joshua gave the order to shout. The first day of the battle finally arrived, and these four groups took their positions at the Jericho wall. They marched around the walls with the priests blowing the horns. On the first day, the walls remained just as impregnable as ever. Nothing visible changed on the second day. The results were the same on the third, fourth, fifth, and sixth days. The priests blew the horns, and the walls stood strong.

However, on the seventh day, they marched around the walls seven times and after the seventh revolution, Joshua said, "Shout! For the LORD has given you the city!" (Joshua 6:16). They shouted before the walls fell, not after the walls fell. This action shows great faith. Hebrews 11:30 records, "By faith the walls of Jericho fell down after being marched around by the Israelites for seven days." God wants us to worship before He works. We must not wait until the battle is over; we must shout, celebrate, and obey God now.

The question remains: How many times will it be necessary for us to march around our Jericho before we realize our dependence on the King? Israel walked thirteen revolutions. How many will we need? Will we need thirty or three hundred? When will believers finally realize that our victory comes by God's Spirit (Zechariah 4:6)? Believers need to be constantly reminded that victory does not lie in our well-thought-out plans but rather in executing the work of the Lord in the way of the Lord revealed by the Spirit of the Lord and found in the Word of the Lord.

Sometimes God's instructions have *when* and *then* components. *When* we do what God has told us to do (obey), *then* we can expect God will do what He said He would do. We have no reason to expect the *then* of God until we have carried out the *when* of our responsibility (obedience). This same order of divine/human instrumentality is evidenced in the New Testament.

When the wine ran out at the wedding in Cana of Galilee, Mary told the servants to obey her son (John 2). Jesus told them to fill six jars with water; they did as instructed; and Jesus did what only He could do. Water does not automatically become wine; however, when Jesus looked at the water, it blushed into wine. In John 11, Lazarus had been dead for four days. No human could resurrect him. Jesus instructed the men to roll back the stone—this they could do. However, Jesus needed to do what only He could do: call Lazarus back to life.

In Luke 5, Peter and others fished all night and caught nothing. They were professional fishermen. They knew where to fish, when to fish, and how to fish. They were coming ashore frustrated after toiling all night to no avail. Jesus told them to go back to the deep (divine instrumentality) and drop their nets (human instrumentality). They obeyed and caught so many fish, they needed assistance with the catch. God is faithful to deliver.

Victory came in Joshua 6:21 after the children of Israel had been obedient. No obedience, no victory. The people destroyed every living thing in Jericho, humans and animals, and saved the valuables to be used in the assembly of the tabernacle. Then, the Lord destroyed the city.

Of Sound or Silence

Review these Bible passages and determine how sound or silence was vital to sensing and responding to God's presence. Categorize them accordingly by checking the box.

	SOUND	SILENCE
Exodus 14:14	☐	☐
Ecclesiastes 3:7	☐	☐
Psalm 9:2	☐	☐
Psalm 37:7	☐	☐
Psalm 46:10	☐	☐
Psalm 47:1	☐	☐
Psalm 150:1-6	☐	☐
Isaiah 30:15	☐	☐
Matthew 21:9	☐	☐
Mark 1:35	☐	☐
1 Thessalonians 4:16	☐	☐
Revelation 19:6	☐	☐

How can you incorporate these elements into your personal worship?

Divine Impact on Human Constructs

Many New Testament prophecies have an Old Testament revelation. The destruction of the walls of Jericho reminds believers of the words of Jesus 1,400 years later in Mark 13:1-2 when Jesus told His disciples the beautiful temple would be destroyed and not one stone would remain on another. Yes, the walls fell down flat (Joshua 6:20).

This catastrophic act had a cataclysmic impact. It would be like watching a thirty-floor, structurally sound building be imploded and instantly reduced from thirty floors to low-lying rubble. This act of God was miraculous. No implosion occurred due to dynamite or the use of a bulldozer, and no earthquake caused it: the hand of God that knocked the walls down flat.

Rahab Was Spared

One question still lingers: How did Rahab and those in her house survive with the walls falling flat? These were huge stones. Joshua 2:15 says Rahab's house was in the city wall. So, if Rahab's house was built within the actual infrastructure of the wall, how did she and her family survive? This may be attributed to *selective demolition.* Perhaps God kept that section of the wall intact and standing while the rest of the wall totally collapsed. Perhaps her house was built within one of the huge stones, and it fell flat intact. In the name of God, the spies assured Rahab that she and her family members who were inside her house would be spared.

We may not ever know how God spared her, but we know He did. We also know that when everything around us falls and caves in, God can spare us from destruction and keep us standing. This is good news for believers: we know God is faithful to establish **His word, His plan and His purpose.** Jericho was a victory of divine/human instrumentality. There was complete participation. Every person went into the city and took the city with the edge of the sword (Joshua 6:20-21).

God gave the Israelites two more instructions. First, valuable metals of silver, gold, brass and iron were to go into the treasury of the Lord to be used in the construction of the tabernacle, which would be in Shiloh. Violating this command would bring a curse on the violator and trouble on the Israelites.

The Company We Keep

The Bible is filled with examples of what may seem like oddities, curiosities, or inexplicable directions from God and nonconformities among His people. Dig into the passages below to learn more about how Christianity often defies norms and conventions.

Unfathomable Authority — Read Isaiah 55:8. What does this tell you about why God's commands may seem illogical or inexplicable?

A Heritage of the Unorthodox — Some translations of 1 Peter 2:9 describe God's chosen as a "peculiar people." Indeed, God's people are so much like Him that they often do not follow human conventions. Read Matthew 3:4 and describe the unusual traits of John the Baptist.

A Deity's Curious Commands — Gideon was not a confident leader like Joshua, but he followed God's strange directions to victory. Read Judges 7 to discover some curiosities about Gideon's defeat of the Midianites. List them here:

The prophet Ezekiel enjoyed a close relationship with God and so obeyed His curious commands. Read Ezekiel 3–4 and record some of the startling actions of the prophet:

What about you? Is there anything in your spiritual conduct that an unbeliever may find peculiar?

Deliverance for All Who Would Believe

The second command could have been more difficult to obey: It required destruction of women, men, boys, girls, babies, and the elderly. Some might question how a just God, the giver of all life, could command the destruction of seemingly innocent people. However, we are reminded to lean not on our own understanding but acknowledge God in all our ways (Proverbs 3:5-6). The command? The only people in Jericho allowed to live were Rahab and the relatives who sought refuge in her house with the scarlet cord hung from the window. Rahab secured their lives because she hid the two messengers who were sent to Jericho by Joshua (6:25). James 2:25 and Hebrews 11:31 emphasize the significance of Rahab's actions. Because of her actions, Rahab and her family were spared!

Joshua did not fight the battle of Jericho alone. It was really Yahweh's battle to fight. Joshua fought the battle only because God allowed him to participate in a fight that was not his to win. Jericho was designated for destruction because of its sin. God had given it, along with the other Amorite cities, four hundred years to turn from sin and to the sovereign God (Genesis 15:16). Jericho received the justice they were due: destruction.

In 6:22, Joshua sent the two spies, who made the promise to Rahab, to go and bring Rahab and all of those in her house out of the city so they could dwell in safety. Apparently, Rahab had been a great evangelist and recruiter for God, because "her father, mother, brothers, and all who belonged to her" were spared because of her evangelistic efforts (Joshua 6:23). God had given her enough time to knock on doors and tell her family members that if they wanted to be saved, they needed to come into the house.

It is most difficult to evangelize the members of our own families. Evidently, they must have seen a tremendous change in her. Evidently, she was not evangelizing them as a person who sold her body and managed a brothel but rather as one who was sold out for God. Evidently, they saw a wonderful change in her, and even though they were pagans who worshiped a myriad of gods, they believed her testimony that God is the God of heaven and earth (Joshua 2:10-11). They were willing to turn to the one true God because Rahab convinced them.

This anticipates the account of the Samaritan woman in John 4. Here was a woman similar to Rahab. She had been married five times and was shacking up with a man when she met Jesus at the well. After being converted, she went back to her hometown and began to evangelize for Jesus (John 4:29). The men went to hear Jesus and, after listening to Him, believed in Him.

Both Rahab and this unnamed woman in John 4 were effective evangelists. To be spared, Rahab's family had to be in her house when Jericho was destroyed. They were not required to be the most ethical, the most spiritual, or the most educated people in the world. They just had to be in the house of the believer, Rahab the prostitute. This is very similar to what took place at the Passover in Egypt. When the death angel came by the house of all the residents in Egypt, the family members of the Jewish household had to be in the house where the doorposts were smeared with the blood of unblemished lambs. Our only security, eternally speaking, is that we have to be in Christ to be spared from eternal damnation.

It is easy to question why a prostitute was spared. However, sober reflection reminds believers that we all have fallen short of God's holy and righteous standard. Similarly, as believers, we all freely receive grace and redemption through Jesus Christ our Lord (Romans 3:23-24). Praise God! We, like Rahab, have been spared. God is faithful to deliver, and in divine human/instrumentality, believers help deliver others through grace, forgiveness, and love.

While God spared Rahab and her family, Romans 8:32 reminds us God "did not even spare His own Son," Jesus Christ, "but gave him up for us all." Isaiah 53:5 tells us He was chastised, wounded, and bruised on our behalf. We are healed by His wounds. In an act of substitutionary atonement, Jesus became sin and was the recipient of death while we who were sinners became recipients of eternal life (Romans 6:23). In essence, Christ became our destruction and death, and we received His grace.

A CLOSER LOOK

Stay Focused

Discerning God's will in certain situations can be quite daunting. Many churches teach believers to stay away from places of ill repute and to avoid people of ill repute. Several churches teach witnessing to those who look like you and talk like you while ignoring those to whom you are categorically dissimilar. However, Jesus talked with a woman at the well, which was not the custom during His day (John 4:4-42). Jesus ate at the house of a tax collector (Matthew 9:10-13). Jesus allowed Mary to wash His feet with her tears and dry them with hair (Luke 7:36-50). Focus on hearing and obeying the voice of God regardless of what others say. Like Ananias, there might be a Paul waiting for your guidance (Acts 9:13-19). Check your perspective.

Application Questions:

1. God's battle plan included marching around a fortress wall thirteen times over seven days without conversation. What do you think would have happened if the Israelites marched around the walls seven times instead? How does faith interact with our actions?

2. Joshua 6 highlights the need for believers to trust God rather than our own understanding. How would you witness to someone questioning the need to obey God meticulously? How could your witness shed light on your personal obedience to God?

3. Divine/human instrumentality gives believers opportunities to invite God's kingdom to come and His will be on earth as it is in heaven. Describe a time when you understood the call to participate in God's plan. What was the outcome?

4. How can God's faithfulness to deliver Rahab and include her in the lineage of His only Son encourage sinners who feel they have no hope or believers who are struggling with faith? What Bible verses would you use to support a witnessing effort that includes the story of Rahab?

5

FAITHFUL TO RENEW

JOSHUA 7-8

Joshua 6 ended with the major chord of victory in honor and fame because the Lord was with Joshua and he was becoming popular in the land (Joshua 6:27). But Joshua 7 begins with a minor chord of dishonor and infamy anticipating defeat because the Israelites were unfaithful to God. There was disobedience in the camp (Joshua 7:1). Seemingly, in the space of one verse, Israel goes from the thrill of victory to the agony of defeat in the eyes of God, and it was because of the sin of one man.

The Israelites assumed they won the battle of Jericho. In reality, they had participated in a march and, at the conclusion of the march, God had dismantled the walls. Then, the Israelite soldiers destroyed the citizens of the city. So, God really fought the battle of Jericho and the walls came tumbling down. The Israelites were about to learn the futility of their strength. **Thankfully, God is faithful to renew.**

Corporate Instructions

When I was a boy, my parents would give my sisters, brother, and me instructions on things to do when they were not at home. Sometimes, we had chores. Other times, we had errands. When my parents returned home, they expected each of us to have done whatever was assigned. They expected absolute obedience from the four of us, as if we all obeyed or disobeyed together. We were rewarded for obedience together or punished for disobedience together. As I reminisce, I realize we were an unofficial ride-or-die quartet.

God had given clear and explicit orders to Joshua for the Israelites to gather valuables from their victory and deposit them in the treasury for the tabernacle and, undoubtedly, for the future construction of the temple. **Joshua assumed his troops complied without fail. He was incorrect.**

Corporate Plans

In chapter 7, the Israelites prepared for their next battle. Joshua sent a recognizance team to Ai to gather intelligence. They came back unimpressed by what they saw. Ai was nothing compared to Jericho. It was much smaller than Jericho with a population of only twelve thousand people in the entire city.[1]

The spies gave a convincing report to Joshua. They were confident a much smaller battle troop could go to fight against and defeat Ai. But their confidence crossed into arrogance. Not only were they confident they would win, they were not prayerful. Joshua acquiesced to their request. After all, their recommendation seemed logical.

Until this time, Joshua got his directions from God, passed them to the leaders, and the leaders transmitted them to the people. The trajectory was from God to His people. But the trajectory here was from God's people to God's people—the leaders did not consult God. Joshua did not pray. Three thousand soldiers were sent to fight against Ai, and they were routed. Thirty-six men were killed. If they were married, thirty-six widows were waiting for husbands who would not return from the battlefield, and children were crying because they were fatherless.

Joshua and the leaders were dismayed. He and the elders fell facedown before the Lord. Joshua lamented that it would have been better for the Israelites to remain on the other side of the Jordan—this sounds like Moses in the desert! Moses and the Israelites saw God cause the death angel to pass over their homes with blood on the doorposts. They saw God allow the death angel to kill the firstborn in the homes without the covering of blood. They knew God caused the Egyptians to make the Israelites wealthy as they sent them out of the land. Yet they longed to return to captivity because Pharaoh, whose firstborn son died like the others, was chasing them (Exodus 14:12).

Joshua cried out, but he was not just concerned about the Israelites. He was concerned about God's reputation. He thought their enemies would hear about their defeat, completely dominate the Israelites in battle, and bring shame and disgrace on the name of Yahweh. After all, God promised him no one would be able to stand against him (Joshua 1:5). Why did this happen?

---

1. Madvig, "Joshua," 284.

Corporate Sin

The same Joshua who led the Israelites around the walls of Jericho, obeying a strange battle plan, leaned on his own understanding for the next war. He did not seek God's guidance. An apparent glaring indictment is his lack of prayer. **Israel's leader did not inspect what God expected from the previous battle.** He did not recognize the presence of sin in the camp. He did not have sight of these failures and sent about three thousand men to go and fight against Ai.

Corporate Punishment

Joshua's decision met with disaster. Thirty-six Israelite soldiers died, and the rest of the army retreated in defeat. When Joshua received the news, he tore his clothes and fell down before the ark of the covenant. The elders also fell down in despair until evening. Joshua and the leaders had made decisions without prayer and had not sought God's instructions in every situation.

God immediately told Joshua to get up. It was not time for a prayer meeting: it was time for a business meeting! The Lord began to give Joshua an explanation for their defeat. Strict orders had been given to the people of God to put all the valuables taken in their victory over Jericho in the treasury to be devoted to the tabernacle that would be built in the future and located in Shiloh. However, one person received the advanced bulletin but ignored it. His name was Achan, an Israelite soldier. He saw a wedge of silver, a nice Babylonian garment, and some gold, and he took it for himself. Achan knew he was violating God's command, so he buried the items in the ground in his tent. This violation was unknown to everyone except the One who sits high, looks low, and sees everything we do. God's eyes were on Achan from the tribe of Judah.

God charged Achan's sin to the entire community of Israel, saying that Israel had sinned, not that Achan had sinned. God considered this a congregational violation. This is similar to Adam's sin. Adam disobeyed God and because of his disobedience, all humanity is born in sin. An innocent animal had to die because blood had to be shed to atone for Adam's sin (Genesis 3:21). This is a picture later seen in the Passover. Innocent lambs died, and their blood covered the sins of Israel, which pointed to the greater Passover Lamb (1 Peter 1:18-21). Believers have symbolically put the blood of the Passover Lamb on our hearts and have been given eternal life (Hebrews 9:12-14). God did not tolerate Achan's sin. If Israel was to move to victory, then the violator, Achan, would need to be discerned and destroyed, along with his family and his possessions. (Of course, God did not tell Joshua the name of the violator).

Every person within the congregation affects the congregation. We live during a time when people tend to individualize their sins and believe what they do only affects them. However, whatever anyone does creates collateral damage and impacts others. A mother who drinks excessively during her pregnancy may very well cause the baby to be born from her womb addicted to alcohol. The challenges this baby might face and the ridicule he or she might suffer at the hands of those who label him or her as a child with challenges are not due to the baby's choices. The mother's choice prompted the potentially devastating domino effect.

Similarly, individuals who are alcoholics or drug addicts affect the entire family who lives with him or her. Even a Christian who is a part of a congregation affects the spiritual temperature of that congregation in a positive or negative sense. In this chapter, God judges the entire nation of Israel based on the sin of one man, Achan. Nehemiah acknowledged that sin is not individual in God's eyes, and he confessed their collective sin to God (Nehemiah 1:6). Daniel also confessed a collective sin to God (Daniel 9:5). Achan's sin was an individual sin, but it had a congregational and national impact. Israel suffered its first loss in the promised land in the first battle against Ai. But God is faithful to renew.

God's Presence and the Ark of the Covenant

It is interesting how defeat can take us right to the foot of the cross where our previously cloudy vision becomes 20/20 and our previous arrogance gets a healthy dose of reality. Israel had gone into battle without the ark of the covenant. It did not make any difference whether Joshua sent three thousand or three hundred thousand Israelites to battle Ai. Israel was destined to lose because God was not with them. There was sin in the camp.

Making Sense of Defeat

Joshua and his people experienced both the thrill of victory and the agony of defeat. In dissecting the defeat at Ai, it becomes clear that Joshua and his army made several missteps and mistakes. Identify one of the critical defeats in your life, such as a job that did not end well, a major purchase that created too much debt, a relationship failure, or something else.

Analyze what went wrong using the following questions:

Did you ask God what to do before making a plan? Y N

Did you wait for His answer? Y N

Did you spiritually prepare yourself before executive God's plan? Y N

Did you do what He said exactly? Y N

Did you actively invoke God's support during the battle? Y N

Despite everything, did you see good come from it? Y N

Would you still call it defeat? Y N

Corporate Renewal Plan

One plus God is not a majority; none plus God is a majority. God is God all by Himself. When He requests divine/human instrumentality, it is not because He needs anyone's assistance. Rather, it is because God blesses us with the opportunity to work within His divine plan. Conversely, if God is against us, no matter what we have by the way of numerical advantage, aesthetic beauty, or financial strength, we will not win. But we can praise God because we have the opportunity to repent, and He promises to renew.

Joshua mirrored Moses in his lamenting and questioning God. Joshua's worldview was subverted and turned upside down. He did not know what to say. He was dumbfounded. Joshua had counted on remaining undefeated because God promised to be with him like He had been with Moses.

Joshua had a greater concern than his own perception: He was concerned with how the nations of Canaan would perceive God after His people were defeated by inconsequential Ai. Would God now be depicted by the nations as weak and no longer have His name considered great due to the failure of His people? **When God's people repent, He is faithful to renew.**

God informed Joshua that Israel's sin resulted in the defeat at Ai. Joshua would deal with the sin situation immediately so God would continue to fight for Israel. God charged to the entire congregation what one man had done singularly. God said Israel stole things devoted to Him and put those things with their own belongings. Even though it was one man who did these things, God charged the sin to the nation. Israel could not stand against their enemies.

God is just. He will demonstrate His wrath on His unrepentant people for sin because He is holy. He is also faithful to renew and gave Joshua instructions to purge the sin from the camp the following day. God gave Joshua a process that exposed the culprit who came forth and was burned in the Valley of Achor, which means "the valley of trouble."[2]

A CLOSER LOOK

Meditate on the Word

In Joshua 7:6, Joshua fell on his face and began questioning God about Israel's military defeat and embarrassment. Joshua did not know Achan had sinned, yet God charged Achan's sin to all Israel. God heard Joshua's inquiry and instructed Joshua to get up and get rid of the sin in the camp.

Hebrews 12:6 reminds us, "for the Lord disciplines the one he loves and punishes every son he receives." As you think about things that happen in your life, good or bad, consider God's faithfulness to renew. When my siblings and I disobeyed our parents, they disciplined us to restore us to proper alignment within the family. God's faithfulness to renew is good news. Submit yourself as a son or daughter to God, willing to be disciplined for His purposes and your good.

---

2. Chad Brand et al., eds., "Achor," in *Holman Illustrated Bible Dictionary* (Nashville, TN: Holman Bible Publishers, 2003), 19.

The Cost of One Man's Sin

God told them to consecrate themselves in preparation for tomorrow. We have heard that word before—"consecrate." In Joshua 3:5, God commanded Joshua to tell the people to consecrate themselves before they crossed over the Jordan River into the promised land. They were to wash and cleanse themselves; they were to separate themselves for God's use; they were to set themselves aside as holy. In Joshua 7, God gives an ultimatum: Israel could not stand in victory against its enemies *until* they had destroyed what brought His judgment on the nation.

God directed Joshua to discern and discover the culprit who had disobeyed God and caused the deaths of thirty-six men. During this process, God offered time and opportunity for confession and repentance. In the morning, all twelve tribes were to be presented. The Lord probably used the casting of lots as a way of showing Joshua who disobeyed God, causing the deaths of thirty-six of his brothers and the defeat of the nation of Israel.

The culprit was from the tribe of Judah, the clan of Zerah, and the family of Zabdi. God led Joshua through the process of elimination. Finally, Achan, from the family of Zabdi, was discovered as the guilty person. A great deal of long-suffering and mercy had been extended to Achan. He could have confessed before the apparent casting of the lots. He could have confessed to God. But he didn't. It was as if Achan had to be smoked out. He was only willing to confess when he got caught. This may be remorse, but it certainly is not repentance. This is similar to Judas in Matthew 27:3 who "was full of remorse" but did not repent.

Achan adopted the three avenues through which sin enters into our lives: the lust of the eyes, the lust of the flesh, and the pride of life (1 John 2:16-17). The lust of the eyes—Achan saw beautiful items; the lust of the flesh—he desired the items; and the pride of life—he took the items and hid them inside his tent. Sin entered into the life of Eve through these same three avenues (Genesis 3:6-7): the lust of the eyes—she saw the fruit; the lust of the flesh—she desired the fruit; the pride of life—she believed the fruit would make her as wise as God. Similarly, sin entered the life of David through the lust of the eyes—David saw Bathsheba bathing; the lust of the flesh—he desired and sent for her; and the pride of life—he took her and laid with her (2 Samuel 11:2-5).

Joshua, along with all the Israelites, took Achan, the valuables he had stolen and hidden, his sons and daughters, livestock, and everything he had to the Valley of Achor. Since he had caused death and defeat for Israel, all of Israel would lead him to the Valley of Achor to witness his destruction and the destruction of all he had.

What we do as individuals affects others, and we see this in Joshua's final pre-execution question: "Why have you brought us trouble?" (v. 25). Once again, this was not simply a singular act that had a singular consequence; it was a singular act that had a national impact. Joshua said that just as Achan had brought trouble on Israel, the Lord would bring trouble on him and his family that day. The people of Israel stoned Achan and his family and then burned their bodies. The ashes of Achan, his family, and livestock were buried under a large pile of rocks. Then, the Lord turned from His anger.

It seems unfair that one person should bring death to his nation and even his own family. Some have even called this a text of terror and suggested that God was unfair. Why should soldiers die and children be cremated for the misdeeds of just one man?

We may not be able to untie the theological knots or to escape the vicissitudes of such a sticky situation. **Our eyes cannot see the degrees of connection God knows.** We cannot fathom the spread of sin among a people started by the mere thought of disobeying. We cannot think highly enough or righteously enough to understand. However, we can consider the greater mystery—the one that took place on a hill and not a valley. It, too, involved something that just does not seem right or fair.

Romans 5:12-21 provides the basis of how God does the unthinkable and even the unreasonable and certainly the inexplicable. It teaches that just as death came into the world by the sin of one man (the first Adam), so righteousness would come through the grace of one man (Christ, the second Adam). Like Achan from the tribe of Judah, Jesus, the second Adam, is also from the tribe of Judah. Achan, the culprit, and Christ, the Savior, are from the same tribe. Achan, the guilty, and Christ, the guiltless, are from the same tribe. Achan, the sinful, and Christ, the sinless, are from the same tribe.

Achan died a shameful death for his sin, and Christ died a shameful death but looked beyond the shame to deliver us from the just penalty for our sin. Achan was from the tribe of Judah; he died as a result of his sin; and his sin affected the entire nation of Israel. Similarly, because the first Adam sinned, all humanity is born into sin.

However, Christ came and paid the price so members of the first Adam's race might be saved. Christ, who is innocent, would die so that the guilty might go free. Christ, who is perfect, would die so the imperfect might be saved. Christ, who is blameless, would be crucified as our kinsman-redeemer so that we, the guilty and the blameworthy, might be redeemed. The selfless act of the second Adam, Jesus, impacted more than just a nation: His sacrifice impacted the entire world. God is faithful to renew!

The singular culprit was Achan—remorseful, but not necessarily repentant. He eventually admitted his sin, but his sin led to death. Like Achan, we were enemies of God—ungodly and hostile to our Creator. Someone had to pay the penalty for our sin and satisfy the righteous demands of God. **Jesus did not die in the Valley of Achor but on a hill and turned the Valley of Achor into a door of hope (Hosea 2:15).**

The Chains that Bind

The Bible is very clear that sin does not happen in a vacuum: the consequences are serious and far reaching. Read each passage below and determine who or what suffered the impact of sin.

Still paying the price: See Genesis 3:14-19 for the legacy of the happenings in the garden of Eden.

Who's sorry now? Read Genesis 6:6 and Isaiah 63:10.

Good and bad news! See Genesis 12:3.

More good and bad news! See Exodus 20:5 and compare the numbers.

No great escape: See Psalm 51:5.

The heavy price He paid: Read Isaiah 53:5.

Toxic waste: Read Psalm 106:38.

When divorce won't divide: See Matthew 5:32.

A word to the unwise: Matthew 18:6-7.

Lest you forget: 1 Corinthians 5:6.

There's hope yet: See Romans 6:23.

A CLOSER LOOK

Stay Focused

God's faithfulness to renew is akin to His holiness. A Hebrew word for holy is *kadosh*. Kadosh means set apart, sinless, and righteous.[3] Scripture admonishes believers to be holy as God is holy. Take a look at 1 Peter 1:15-16, "But as the one who called you is holy, you also are to be holy in all your conduct; for it is written, **Be holy, because I am holy.**" We will not be perfect. However, we can focus on being holy as God is holy.

Corporate Victory

Joshua 8 introduces the ruse or the victory through deception over the people of Ai. Recovering lost ground is difficult but necessary. It's hard to go back to those broken places in life and seek to have them mended. It's hard to revisit broken relationships and seek to have them restored. It's hard to face Ai where one has lost thirty-six men, and lost the battle, and win the victory this time. But we must go back.

---

3. Strong, *A Concise Dictionary*, 102.

Professional teams watch film after a loss to see what was done wrong in the game so they can learn from their mistakes and hopefully be victorious when they play the same team again. After watching the film of the battle of Ai, Israel discovered several reasons for their defeat:

1. They did not consult God in prayer.
2. They underestimated the enemy in a place much smaller than Jericho.
3. They were overconfident in their ability.
4. They did not know there was someone in the camp who had violated the covenant of God.

Israel would use a new strategy this time—deception! Who would authorize this strategy? God Himself! Isn't God a God of veracity? Isn't deception contradictory to truth? God is faithful to renew and can **predictively recycle deception and use it for His divine purpose.** The greatest demonstration of this is Calvary. The death of Jesus resulted in deliverance and salvation for sinners who would believe. Death to themselves in Christ resulted in renewed life in Christ!

The victory was guaranteed by God, who had **handed** to Israel the king of Ai and its citizens just as He had **handed over** the city Jericho. In both instances, God says to Joshua, "I have handed [them] over to you" (Joshua 6:2; 8:1). The Israelites were to deposit the devoted valuables into the treasury of the Lord after their victory in Jericho. After their victory in Ai, they were permitted to keep the valuables and livestock for themselves.

Here was the military strategy: Ambush! God fought for Israel through their obedience, and they won. People in the city came out of hiding; the Israelites seized Ai and set it on fire. The soldiers of Ai who had been drawn away looked back and saw smoke rising from their city. It was too late to return to the city, for Joshua's troops surrounded them from all directions. Ai's soldiers were trapped and totally defeated. Not one survivor remained, except the king of Ai who was brought to Joshua. His body was hung on a tree until evening and was then thrown down and covered up with a large pile of rocks, just like the pile of rocks that covered Achan's body. **A renewal ceremony took place after the victory. God is faithful to renew!**

After the victory, God scheduled a service of consecration and dedication. An altar was built, and sacrifices were offered on it. Among the sacrifices was the burnt offering, in which the entire animal was burned. It represented what God wanted from each Israelite: wholehearted devotion. This anticipates Paul's words in Romans 12:1, imploring believers to present ourselves as living sacrifices. Christ offered His whole self to God, and He gave Himself as a peace offering (Romans 5:1). We are in fellowship with God. It is not just a status (peace) but an activity (fellowship).

All of Israel stood facing the ark of the covenant, representing the presence of God among His people. Joshua read from the law of God to keep the people connected with the Word of God so they could remain connected with the God of the Word. Some of the people stood in front of Mount Ebal. This area had a high acoustical capacity. Futher, Mount Ebal represented curses. If they disobeyed this law, they would reap the curses of Mount Ebal. Some stood in front of Mount Gerizim, which represented blessings. Those who obeyed the law would reap blessings. These two mountains pointed to Jesus and to us. Jesus, who is the personification of Mount Gerizim, becomes Mount Ebal, and we who are born in sin and shaped in iniquity (Mount Ebal) become Mount Gerizim (2 Corinthians 5:17-19).

Application Questions:

1. Joshua 6 ended with a high, and Joshua 7 began with a low. Describe a time when you celebrated a high only to rebound with a crushing blow? How did your faith help you endure your situation?

2. God gave military strategies to Joshua and often instructed the Israelites to completely annihilate those they defeated. How would you explain God's holiness to those who do not understand God's judgment?

3. Define spiritual renewal. How does God's promise to renew give you encouragement for your journey?

6

GOD IS FAITHFUL TO ESTABLISH

JOSHUA 12-22

Good movies have excellent side stories about which viewers are given pertinent information in the twists and turns of the action. The book of Joshua is like one of those movies, except its background information covers several chapters that seem boring: they are not. Certainly, these chapters fall short of actual dramatic events like parting waters, falling walls, burning cities, extension of light, delay of night, and hurled hailstones. **However, these chapters steadfastly communicate that God is faithful to establish His people, His plans, and His ways.**

Joshua 1 began with God's cataclysmic announcement that Moses, the mediator of an important covenant between the tribes, was dead. Through Moses, the Lord promised that if the two and a half tribes of Reuben, Gad, and the half tribe of Manasseh would share in the conflict with their brothers of the nine and a half tribes on the east side, He would give them the land promised to them on the wilderness side of the Jordan. Now, Moses was dead and the covenant between the two and a half tribes and their brothers hung in the balance.

Some promises and covenants are unconditional—like the Noahic covenant in which God promised that the world would never again be destroyed by flood (Genesis 9:11). However, the covenant with the two and a half tribes is a conditional covenant contingent on the tribes doing their part in fighting with their fellow tribes until Canaan had rest from war. Like these tribes, it is important for believers to not only begin ministry well but also finish ministry well.

In Joshua 1:12-18, these two and a half tribes renewed their commitment under Joshua to fight in the promised land until Israel took control and all territorial lots and inheritances were assigned (Numbers 32). Joshua chapters 12–22 articulate the significance of past experiences with God providing present confidence in God. Whenever Israel faced a challenge, they could always look back and remember God is faithful to establish His people and His word.

Failure to Possess Their Full Possession

Israel had some success in the promised land. However, the Lord reminded Joshua of unpossessed and unclaimed territories. Though God had given the entire land to the Israelites, there were promised territories the Israelites failed to make their own. The Israelites did not drive out all nations inhabiting Canaan. **The list is an indictment of Israel's failure to possess unclaimed possessions and unclaimed territories** (Joshua 13:13; 15:63; 16:10; 17:12).

In addition to these territories that were still in the hands of the original dwellers (13:3-6), there were other unpossessed territories occupied by the Canaanite enemies of Israel. Only the two and a half tribes who chose to set up residence in the land on the east side of the Jordan had received their territorial inheritance. The nine and a half tribes of Israel who would live on the west side of the Jordan were still waiting to receive their land allotment—and Joshua was to be the Secretary of Housing. He was to apportion lots to the nine and a half tribes. It was time for God to establish His people.

Awarding Land Allotments

In chapter 14, Joshua began gifting territories, and an octogenarian (someone eighty years of age or older), Caleb, stepped up. What a vote of confidence and faith in God's faithfulness to establish! A nearly seven-year military engagement in Canaan was over. (Israel left Egypt and came to Mount Sinai, remaining there for one or two years to receive instruction from God regarding how they were to live once they got into the promised land. After the training/orientation was over, the children of Israel wandered in the wilderness for thirty-eight years. So, that's one to two years at Mount Sinai, thirty-eight years wandering around in the wilderness, and seven years to conquer the land of Canaan: finally settling into the promised land was about forty-seven years in the making!)[1]

---

1. Madvig, "Joshua," 324.

Moses had promised territory to Caleb before the military campaign in Canaan, before the end of the journey in the wilderness, and before Moses was given a private burial by God (Numbers 14:24; Deuteronomy 34:5-6). The promise was made in the name of God. Caleb and Moses did not know when the Israelites would move into the land of promise, Canaan, and take control. They knew God had given them the land, and they believed God is faithful to establish His word. It was the ultimate expression of faith. Forty-six to forty-seven years later, Caleb stepped up first to receive his promised possession.

How long can we wait on the promise of God to be fulfilled in our lives? Whether it has been four years, forty years, or forty-seven years since God made the promise, you can believe He is faithful to establish it. **God is not in time; time is in God.** If God said it, He will do it. God is faithful to establish His word and faithful to put people in our lives who can encourage and strengthen us on our journey.

Caleb and Joshua were about the same age and were now octogenarians. Both demonstrated the blessings that come when we serve God faithfully while waiting for Him to establish His will in our lives. They had been serving God together a long time in their individual assignments without reports of jealousy or sabotage. Believers should work together for God's purposes in the same way. Each of us has a part to do.

On January 15, 2009, Captain Chesley "Sully" Sullenberger left New York's LaGuardia Airport on US Airways Flight 1549 with 155 passengers and crew on board. Within minutes of takeoff, a flock of Canadian geese flew into the twin engines of the plane, immobilizing them and leaving the plane without power. Captain Sullenberger was able to steer the plane and avoid crashing into buildings. He also flew the plane nine hundred feet over the George Washington Bridge and safely landed it on the Hudson River. One hundred and fifty-five passengers and crew members boarded the plane at LaGuardia, and one hundred and fifty-five exited onto the plane's wings on the Hudson. There were no casualties. Sully got most of the accolades for his aviation maneuvers and astuteness.[2] However, he remarked that he could not have done this by himself. While he was flying the plane, his copilot, Jeff Skiles, was flipping switches and adjusting flaps to optimize the plane's position for its best chance to land safely.

---

2. Angelica Stabile, "On this day in history, January 15, 2009, US Airways flight makes miraculous landing in the Hudson River," Fox News, January 15, 2024, https://www.foxnews.com/lifestyle/this-day-history-jan-15-2009-us-airways-flight-makes-landing-hudson-river.

The sons of Joseph, the eleventh son of Jacob and former vice-regent of Egypt, were among the tribes receiving allotments. Ephraim and Manasseh enjoyed the blessings of being Jacob's adopted sons and their father Joseph's sons. Through Joseph's revelation and interpretation of the Pharaoh's dream, grain was saved and the Egyptians were sustained throughout a seven-year famine. Not only were the Egyptians sustained because of the stored grain, but Joseph's eleven brothers, his father, and his family—seventy people in total—got grain from Egypt and were spared from starvation. All of this took place because God is faithful to establish His people and His purpose.

What areas and possibilities remain unclaimed and unpossessed in your life, work, and ministry? What doors have you failed to enter, and what mountains do you refuse to tunnel through? What talents and gifts remain undeveloped? It is not too late. Joshua lived to be 110 years old (Joshua 24:29). He lived a life of faithfulness to God. "Moses was one hundred twenty years old when he died; his eyes were not weak, and his vitality had not left him" (Deuteronomy 34:7). Caleb testified of his strength at age eighty-five: he was as strong then as he was when Moses sent them out on the first mission (Joshua 14:11). Caleb had been waiting for forty-seven years to receive his land inheritance. As one of the two faithful spies (Joshua being the other), Caleb undoubtedly saw the land of Hebron about forty-five years earlier, yet he waited patiently for God to establish him in the land. Believers must strive to be consistently faithful so we do not leave behind an unfinished past. We can learn to trust God and wait as long as it takes (Psalm 27:14). He will establish what He has promised, just as He did for Caleb.

Caleb was from the tribe of Judah. He condescended and served as second fiddle to Joshua. However, Caleb was not second fiddle to himself. He did what God assigned him to do. There is another leader from the tribe of Judah: Jesus. He condescended and took on the form of a man like Caleb, and according to Philippians 2:5-11, did not consider equality with God as something to be exploited. Instead he emptied Himself. As a servant, Jesus was "obedient to the point of death, even to death a cross" (v. 8). Unlike Caleb, who died and remained in the grave, Jesus rose from the dead on the third day. God gives believers an eternal inheritance through Christ in the power of the Spirit (Ephesians 1:13-14). He is faithful to lead and will raise Caleb and all believers one day for the heavenly Mount Zion where death will die and tears will be no more.

The tribe of Levi did not receive land allotments because their responsibility was to take care of the holy things of God. However, God designated forty-eight cities throughout Canaan as places for Levites to reside and care for their herds. God chose Levi as the sole tribe from which the priests would be selected. Not all of the men from the tribe of Levi became priests, but all of the priests were from the tribe of Levi. Levitical priests took care of tabernacle furnishings and led worship for the pilgrims during the mandatory feasts and festivals. They received something better than a territorial allotment: God promised to be their portion. The congregation would provide food for the Levites through their meat offerings and other offerings given to God.

Cities of Refuge

God, who is all-knowing, knew there would be internal strife and conflict within the tribes of Israel and preemptively established cities of refuge. Even after achieving much success against other nations by the hand of God, the Israelites were prone to have problems within their own camps. Many believers can identify with the Israelites and Paul. We want to do good, but the enemy's influence impacts our actions (Romans 7:21). God established a solution for the inevitable problem of personal and interpersonal conflict and strife.

Just as he did during Moses's administration, the Lord told Joshua to designate cities of refuge. Cities of refuge were places of safety and asylum for individuals who unintentionally take a life. The homicide could not be premeditated, intentional, or purposeful for the perpetrator to have a chance of being protected. The offender could run to one of six cities of refuge (three on the east and three on the west) and find safety there from the avenger of blood, a family member of the deceased seeking to avenge his relative's death. If the avenger of blood apprehended the offender before he was admitted to a city of refuge, then the avenger of blood was cleared of any charge. Once admitted to a city of refuge, the perpetrator had to remain in the city until the high priest died. The perpetrator could then be released.

We are all offenders (Romans 3:23), and we run to our refuge, Jesus Christ. He is our high priest and our ark of safety (Hebrews 7:25). **We must remain in Him, for He lives forever.** He died once, never to die again. His death and resurrection guarantee our eternal security.

An impartial process was established to determine if an offender was allowed to enter the city. After listening to the offender's plea, the city's elders would weigh its sincerity and veracity. If they admitted the offender, they would provide him a place to live with them. It was an act of grace. Similarly, more openness and forgiveness can help churches be safe places and avoid being guilty of unjustly ostracizing or criminalizing people.

Promise Made, Promises Kept?

Joshua noted that God fully kept His promises to the Israelites, but some of them took a long time for fulfillment. A promise delayed is often about our own failure to live up to our side of the bargain. Review the promises below and decide if it's conditional on our participation and obedience and whether it's been fulfilled or if you are still waiting.

BIBLE REFERENCE	CONDITIONAL	STATUS
Genesis 9:11	☐ Yes ☐ No	☐ Fulfilled ☐ In Progress
Deuteronomy 31:6	☐ Yes ☐ No	☐ Fulfilled ☐ In Progress
Deuteronomy 31:8	☐ Yes ☐ No	☐ Fulfilled ☐ In Progress
Psalm 37:4	☐ Yes ☐ No	☐ Fulfilled ☐ In Progress
Proverbs 3:5-6	☐ Yes ☐ No	☐ Fulfilled ☐ In Progress
Proverbs 22:6	☐ Yes ☐ No	☐ Fulfilled ☐ In Progress
Isaiah 40:31	☐ Yes ☐ No	☐ Fulfilled ☐ In Progress
Matthew 6:31-33	☐ Yes ☐ No	☐ Fulfilled ☐ In Progress
Mark 11:24	☐ Yes ☐ No	☐ Fulfilled ☐ In Progress
John 10:10	☐ Yes ☐ No	☐ Fulfilled ☐ In Progress
John 14:15-17	☐ Yes ☐ No	☐ Fulfilled ☐ In Progress
Romans 8:28	☐ Yes ☐ No	☐ Fulfilled ☐ In Progress
James 1:5	☐ Yes ☐ No	☐ Fulfilled ☐ In Progress
James 4:7	☐ Yes ☐ No	☐ Fulfilled ☐ In Progress

Crossing the River

Once the territorial lots had been assigned, the battle fought and the victory won, the two and a half tribes were ready to go back home. Joshua gave them a wonderful send-off. He gave them clothes, precious metals, and livestock because they had been faithful and lived up to their covenant of brotherhood.

A CLOSER LOOK

Meditate on the Word

After crossing the Jordan River to possess their land, the two and a half tribes built a memorial to establish proof of their participation in securing the promised land. The nine and a half tribes misunderstood the purpose of the project and were prepared to fight to protect themselves against the wrath of God. Both acts reveal a lack of trust among family members.

Contrastingly, David and Jonathan trusted one another even though Jonathan's father, King Saul, wanted to kill David. First Samuel 18:1 reveals Jonathan loved David as he loved himself. These friends trusted each other like brothers and demonstrated great love.

Believers are instructed to trust in the Lord and not rely on our own understanding (Proverbs 3:5-6). We are similarly instructed to be known by our love for one another (John 13:35). Reflect on your commitment to trust God's plan and work in your life and in the lives of other believers.

Trouble Among God's People

Then, a crisis broke out. Word got out that the tribes on the east side of the Jordan River had built an imposing altar at Geliloth near the river. It was such a monumental altar that it could be seen from either side of the river. Trouble was brewing at the river. When the nine and a half tribes on the west side of the river heard that the other two and a half tribes had built this imposing altar, they decided to go to war (Joshua 22:11-12). They understood from Achan's story that if one tribe violated God's law, all tribes would have violated His law and would face judgment.

They intended to fight against Reuben, Gad, and the half tribe of Manasseh. What a tragedy! If this happened, the half tribe of Manasseh on the west side of the Jordan and the half tribe of Manasseh on the east side of the Jordan would fight each other. Blood relatives would fight each other.

Collaboration and Communication Conquers Confusion

When they arrived, Phinehas challenged them about the altar built in an undesignated place. According to Deuteronomy 12:5-7, no altar should be built for sacrifice in a place undesignated by God, and God had designated Shiloh. Phinehas reminded the tribes of their history and accused them of unfaithfulness, but God is faithful to establish.

Toward the end of the chapter (22:22-29), the leaders of the two and a half tribes spoke up, essentially saying, "We know there's only one designated place to build an altar for sacrifice, but we didn't build this altar for sacrifice. We built this altar for a memorial because we know how subject we all are to amnesia. We do not want you to write us out of our history. We do not want our children growing up and being told that the nine and a half tribes are the only tribes that took control of the land and drove out the enemies and that the two and a half tribes had no part in it. If they believe that story, then they will be susceptible to idolatry. We know how forgetful we are. In fact, we are so forgetful that one of us from each of the twelve tribes of Israel took a stone out of the Jordan River and piled them up for a memorial on the eastern side in the city of Gilgal, the headquarters of Israel. We did that because we wanted our children to know what the stones mean. We want our children to know our God is powerful and faithful to establish."

The delegation from the nine and a half tribes listened to those who represented the two and a half tribes and heard what they said. Earlier, they had heard rumors (22:11). Then they heard perceptions. But finally, they heard from the mouths of the people who knew the facts, and they were pleased (22:31). They essentially concluded, "The Lord is with us because He kept us from slaughtering our brothers and committing mutual homicide."

When they returned home to Joshua and the nine and a half tribes, they reported what they had heard. Then, they named the altar a witness between them and God (22:34).

What is God saying to us? Is He saying something to us about what He can do when we are on the verge of theological mutual homicide? Perhaps God is saying that we need to participate in a collaboration. Too many believers give too many monologues and do not have enough dialogues. Too many believers give many diagnoses but not enough prescriptions. We need an incarnational approach.

Jesus is the Word who "became flesh and dwelt among us. We observed his glory, the glory as the one and only Son from the Father, full of grace and truth" (John 1:14). Eugene Peterson's paraphrase of what John said in John 1:14 is, "The Word became flesh and blood, and moved into the neighborhood" (MSG). Further, as Clarence Jordan said in the *Cotton Patch* version of 2 Corinthians 5:19, "God was in Christ, hugging the world to himself."[3]

These guard gates must come down. Believers must collaborate. We must talk to one another. However, we should not compromise our convictions. The nine-and-a-half-tribe delegation and the representatives of the two and a half tribes talked together. They did not compromise convictions about Scripture. When the Bill of Rights and the Bible collide, we must be directed by the Bible. When Capitol Hill and the hill far away collide, we must be directed by Calvary. When the flag and the cross collide, we must choose the cross. When government and God collide, we must choose God, because the kingdoms of this world will "become the kingdom of our Lord and of his Christ, and he will reign forever and ever" (Revelation 11:15b). When the White House and the *right house* of John 14:2 collide, we must be choose the *right house*. Jesus came to reconcile us to God. We were separated from God: we were His enemies. Jesus became sin for us when He had no sin in Him so we can be the righteousness of God (2 Corinthians 5:21). As a result, we are exhorted to be ministers of reconciliation (2 Corinthians 5:18-20). We do not compromise our convictions. We choose those God has been faithful to establish.

---

3. Clarence Jordan, *The Cotton Patch Gospel: Paul's Epistles* (Macon: Smyth & Helwys Publishing, 2004), 76.

Safe Spaces

The Bible uses several images to describe the protection and refuge we may seek in God. Read the verses below and match them to the appropriate word. One verse or passage may contain more than one allegory.

2 Samuel 22:3	shadow
Psalm 17:8	fortress
Psalm 18:2	horn
Psalm 27:5	shield
Psalm 61:3	wings
Psalm 91:1	rock
Psalm 121:1-3	stronghold
Proverbs 30:5	shelter
Isaiah 4:6	strong tower
Nahum 1:7	anchor
Hebrews 6:18-19	mountains
	shade

A CLOSER LOOK

Stay Focused

God makes a great promise in Isaiah 55:11: "So my word that comes from my mouth will not return to me empty, but it will accomplish what I please and will prosper in what I send it to do." Like the two and a half tribes, believers must be willing to hold on to the promises of God and work within divine/human instrumentality to bring those promises to pass. Like the nine and a half tribes, believers must diligently guard their hearts to do all that God requires and lovingly correct error that can incur the wrath of God. Hold on to God's promises. He is faithful to establish His word and His people.

Application Questions

1. Second Timothy 3:16–17 teaches, "All Scripture is inspired by God and is profitable for teaching, for rebuking, for correcting, for training in righteousness, so that the man of God may be complete, equipped for every good work." How do you remain faithful to this truth when studying texts like Joshua 12–22? What techniques would you teach those new to Bible study? What warnings would you give to encourage accurate interpretation of the text?

2. The two and a half tribes asked for desirable land on the other side of the Jordan River, outside of the promised land. Reconcile the tribes' request with the believer's desire to pursue God's best. How does trust impact a believer's reconciliation of having a personal preference and knowing God has designated a more perfect gift?

3. The nine and a half tribes prepared to go to war with the two and a half tribes over a misunderstanding. How can believers employ Phinehas's wise actions to inform handling of church disputes or misunderstandings between brothers and sisters in Christ?

4. Regarding biblical reconciliation, how can Joshua 12–22 guide discussions of compromise versus collaboration?

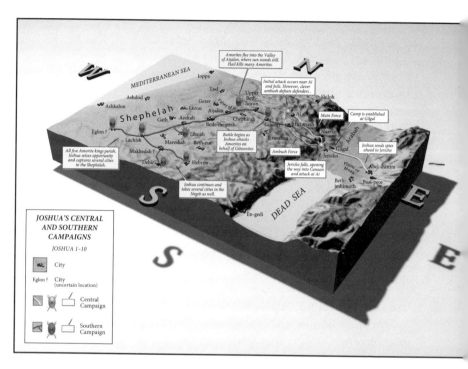

Amorites flee into the Valley of Aijalon, where sun stands still. Hail kills many Amorites.

Initial attack occurs near Ai and fails. However, clever ambush defeats defenders.

Main Force

Camp is established at Gilgal

Joshua sends spies ahead to Jericho

Battle begins as Joshua attacks Amorites on behalf of Gibeonites

Ambush Force

Jericho falls, opening the way into Canaan and attack at Ai

All five Amorite kings perish. Joshua seizes opportunity and captures several cities in the Shephelah.

Joshua continues and takes several cities in the Negeb as well.

MEDITERRANEAN SEA

Shephelah

DEAD SEA

JOSHUA'S CENTRAL AND SOUTHERN CAMPAIGNS

JOSHUA 1–10

City

Eglon ?   City (uncertain location)

Central Campaign

Southern Campaign

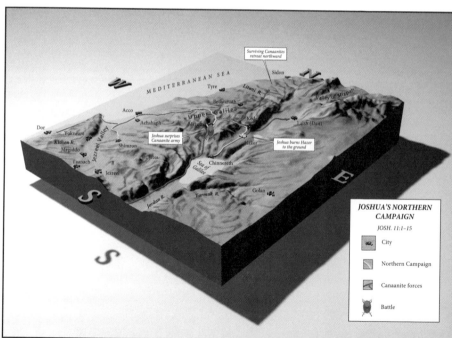

Surviving Canaanites retreat northward

Joshua surprises Canaanite army

Joshua burns Hazor to the ground

MEDITERRANEAN SEA

Upper Galilee

Jezreel Valley

Sea of Galilee

JOSHUA'S NORTHERN CAMPAIGN

JOSH. 11:1–15

City

Northern Campaign

Canaanite forces

Battle

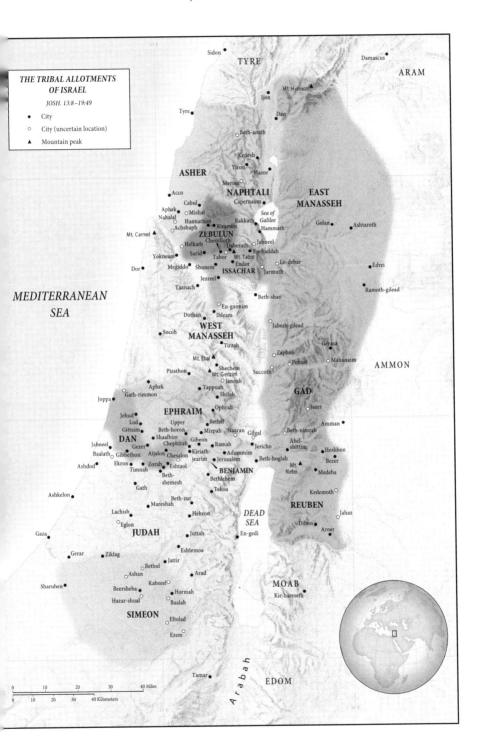

THE TRIBAL ALLOTMENTS OF ISRAEL

JOSH. 13:8–19:49

● City
○ City (uncertain location)
▲ Mountain peak

Sidon

TYRE

Damascus

ARAM

Mt. Hermon ▲

Ijon

Tyre

Dan

Beth-anath

Kedesh

Yiron

Hazor

ASHER

Merom

NAPHTALI

EAST MANASSEH

Acco

Cabul

Capernaum

Aphek

Mishal

Nahalal

Hannathon

Rakkath

Sea of Galilee

Golan

Ashtaroth

Achshaph

Rimmon

Hammath

ZEBULUN

Helkath

Chesulloth

Daberath

Jabneel

Yokneam

Sarid

Tabor

Mt. Tabor ▲

En-haddah

Lo-debar

Edrei

Dor

Megiddo

Shunem

Endor

Jarmuth

Ramoth-gilead

ISSACHAR

Jezreel

Taanach

Beth-shan

En-gannim

Dothan

Ibleam

Jabesh-gilead

WEST MANASSEH

Socoh

Tirzah

Gerasa

Zaphon

Mt. Ebal ▲

Penuel

Mahanaim

Pirathon

Shechem

Mt. Gerizim ▲

Succoth

AMMON

Janoah

Aphek

Tappuah

Gath-rimmon

Shiloh

GAD

Joppa

Ophrah

EPHRAIM

Jehud

Upper

Bethel

Jazer

Lod

Beth-horon

Mizpah

Naaran

Gilgal

Amman

Gittaim

Shaalbim

Gibeon

Ramah

Beth-nimrah

DAN

Gezer

Chephirah

Jericho

Abel-shittim

Heshbon

Jabneel

Aijalon

Chesalon

Kiriath-jearim

Adummim

Bezer

Baalath

Gibbethon

Beth-hoglah

Ashdod

Ekron

Zorah

Eshtaol

Jerusalem

Mt. Nebo ▲

Medeba

Timnah

Beth-shemesh

BENJAMIN

Bethlehem

Gath

Tekoa

Kedemoth

Beth-zur

REUBEN

Ashkelon

Mareshah

Lachish

Hebron

DEAD SEA

Jahaz

Eglon

Juttah

En-gedi

Dibon

Aroer

Gaza

JUDAH

Eshtemoa

Gerar

Ziklag

Jattir

Arad

MOAB

Bethul

Kir-hareseth

Ashan

Kabzeel

Sharuhen

Beersheba

Hormah

Hazar-shual

Baalah

SIMEON

Eltolad

Ezem

Tamar

Arabah

EDOM

MEDITERRANEAN SEA

0   10   20   30   40 Miles
0   10   20   30   40 Kilometers

7

FAITHFUL TO HIS PROMISES

JOSHUA 23-24

On August the 24, 1995, I gave my farewell sermon at the New Mission Baptist Church of Cincinnati, Ohio. This was the church of my teenage years. This was the church that ordained me as a minister of the gospel. This was the church that called me their Senior Pastor. This was the church where I had been married and the church where my children were dedicated to the Lord. Now, after nearly twenty years of pastoral service, I was giving my final sermon and making the transition to a full-time professorship at the Southern Baptist Theological Seminary in Louisville, Kentucky.

I had been ecstatic about the *invocation* of my ministry there, and I was saddened about the *benediction* ending of my ministry there. I loved the church, and the church loved me. But my work was done; I had finished my course. God had been faithful to His promises at New Mission and had revealed new promises and a new mission to me. I could look back over my life and know God would be faithful.

I also cared very deeply about the life of the congregation. I wanted them to know God would lead and guide them. I wanted them to remember God's faithfulness through the years was not a one-time blessing. God would continue to be faithful to His promise. The congregation would need to follow God's new leader and trust God for their direction and protection.

Recount God's Faithfulness

In chapter 23, Joshua is a very old man who served Israel well. He and Caleb had been faithful spies; they gave a faithful report about the nation's ability to take the land of Canaan with the help of the Lord. He had served as a faithful assistant under Moses for nearly forty years; he had been a faithful leader who led the nation out of the wilderness into the promised land; and he had been the faithful military commander of Israel's armed forces. He distributed the territorial allotments to the tribes according to God's directions. He had retired from active duty and was now coming out of retirement to give his final address and final instructions to his beloved Israel.

Joshua delivered a theocentric address for the elders, judges, and officials. His address was *God-centered* and not anthropocentric, *human-centered*. **Listeners could not help but hear redemptive reverberations resounding throughout the course of his address concerning what God had done on the behalf of Israel.** He reminded Israel:

- "And you have seen for yourselves everything the LORD *your God* did to all these nations on your account" (23:3a). He is faithful to His promises.
- "It was the LORD *your God* who was fighting for you" (23:3b).
- "The LORD *your God* will force them back on your account and drive them out before you so that you can take possession of their land, as the LORD *your God* promised you" (23:5).
- "*The* LORD has driven out great and powerful nations before you" (23:9a).
- "None of the good promises the LORD *your God* made to you has failed" (23:14b).

Joshua was about to go the way of all the earth and wanted to leave Israel with some extremely important instructions and admonitions. They were to be obedient to the book of the law given to Moses by God without turning to the right or to the left (23:6). This is the same instruction God gave Joshua at the very beginning of his ministry to Israel as their leader (1:7). They were not to fraternize with the nations who remained in the promised land, lest they adopt their idolatrous worldview and lifestyle. They were to be very intentional about loving God, the second action commanded of Israel by God in the Shema (Deuteronomy 6:4-9). They were to be *set apart* as God's people from the surrounding nations and refrain from fraternizing with them to avoid becoming like them. After this, Joshua had one final assignment. He must give instructions to the assembled congregation and children at Shechem.

Shechem is a very important place in the history of Israel. When Abraham left Ur of the Chaldeans, he arrived in Canaan at a place called Shechem (Genesis 12:6). Joshua told the gathered Israelites to renew the covenants of the Lord. He rehearsed Israel's redemptive history, hoping the one thing they had learned from their history was that they *had learned* from their history. He knew Israel had not learned. He knew Israel had fits and episodes of amnesia. Israel was unfaithful, but Joshua recounted God's faithfulness to keep His promises.

Joshua knows the people. He knows it is necessary to rehearse Israel's history before this congregation. Some of the men listening had experienced Egypt as young boys and had seen the wonders of God. Others had only heard about the great things God had done because they were born in the promised land. Undoubtedly, many teenagers were in the congregation at that time as well as adolescents and small children. They all needed to know their responsibility to worship and serve God, a concept prolifically referenced in Joshua 24 (vv. 14-15,18-22,24,31).

Joshua retold their history meticulously. He presented Israel in their pre-Canaan existence with Terah and brought them through time. He gave an audio rerun of how God delivered them from Egyptian oppression and delivered Moses from an early grave while later delivering Pharaoh and his Egyptian army to a watery grave in the Red Sea. He recounted Israel's great crossing of the Jordan River and the defeat of the seven nations occupying the promised land—a land they did not labor for, with cities they did not build and vineyards and olive groves they did not plant.

It is of paramount significance for youth and the aged to talk about the mighty acts of God. In fact, Deuteronomy 6:7 admonishes fathers (parents) to talk about God and His Word to their children "when you sit in your house and when you walk along the road, when you lie down and when you get up." Adults recount and retell the story to encourage one another and to teach the children.

Believers must be eyewitnesses who tell the story of what God has done in their lives. We must not be tied to the apron strings of our parents when it comes to salvation, for God does not have a salvation family plan. **God has no grandchildren: He only has children. We must know God for ourselves.**

A CLOSER LOOK

Stay Focused

Observant members of the Jewish faith say the Shema (Deuteronomy 6:4-9) at least three times a day. It is one of the earliest Scriptures they teach their children. It establishes the parental responsibility to teach children the ways of the Lord throughout the day in various situations to immerse them in God's commands. Examine the biblical connectedness and spiritual legacy you are building in your family. Repetition, respect, and reverence are taught throughout the book of Joshua.

Revere God's Faithfulness

Joshua admonished Israel to "fear the LORD and worship him in sincerity and truth" (24:14). Pockets of enemy nations remained in the land, and various idol gods remained in their hearts. In spite of all God had done for Israel, they still held onto gods that their ancestors served in the region of Ur of the Chaldeans and in Egypt, as well as the gods of the Amorites in whose land they were living. However, Joshua, knowing he could not bring about a decision on the part of the nation, made an announcement for his own house: "As for me and my family, we will worship the LORD" (Joshua 24:15). He had seen God work and knew Him to be faithful to His promises.

His statement is etched in wood, written on the finest of paper, and hung as placards and posters on the walls of homes. But these words are meant to emerge through the pores of believers' hearts who are fully surrendered to serving the Lord. The word "serve" registers the pulsating heartbeat of this passage. It is found 16 times in this chapter (verse 2, 3 times in v. 14, 5 times in verse 15 and in verses 16, 18, 19, 20, 21, 22, 24, and 31). The Israelites considered it nonsense to even suggest a possibility of their returning to idolatry and abandoning their service to the Lord. God was their deliverer from Egyptian bondage, sustainer, preserver, and miracle worker through their trek through the wilderness to the promised land.

Set Apart

Joshua's cautions to the Israelites to remain holy and wholly devoted to God align with other teachings throughout the Bible. **Review the two examples below and paraphrase:**

2 Corinthians 6:14-18

James 4:4

With a shallow reading, one may assume believers join an exclusive club that rejects outsiders, but that's not necessarily true. See the passages below to discover the high calling to be a follower of Jesus Christ.

Romans 8:9: Their lives are not our own; not even their bodies. The _____ of God dwells within believers, and He is not an unassuming resident but works in each believer to help him or her become more Christ-like.

Romans 12:2: Believers make decisions and experience renewal through a process that mystifies the outside world: the _____ of our _____. They employ prayer and the Word.

Colossians 4:5: Their responsibility to unbelievers is not to reject, degrade, or hate, but to act _____ toward them and to be ready to share God and their stories with them.

1 Peter 2:9: Followers of Jesus are uniquely tasked to _____ the praises of God, and it requires consistency, sincerity, and passion.

1 John 5:18: Christians are called to be morally upright, even in thought. They repent of and abstain from _____.

To paraphrase their answer to Joshua in verses 16-18, "Don't even give a single thought to us not serving the Lord and serving idols instead. We will stand firm and sure in obedience!"

The people reiterated their position and resoundingly agreed with Joshua's historical observation. It was the Lord who had been Israel's deliverer throughout their history. They would be faithful and serve the Lord, because God had been faithful to them. Joshua knew his people, like good leaders do. Joshua responded with a seemingly inappropriate and inaccurate statement about God's character and action. God is a God of long suffering, mercy, and second chances. Israel's history had proven this. Throughout their history, Israel had been the beneficiary of God's benevolence, forgiveness, and restoration. But Joshua told them they could not serve the Lord! He even told them God would not forgive their sins and transgressions when God had forgiven them for past generations (vv. 19-20). Hadn't he just told the story?

Joshua was not talking about permissibility, he was talking about the nature of God and nature of his people. God would not tolerate unholiness and insincerity because He is a holy and jealous God. Holiness is the essence of who God is. God is wholly other, righteous and just. He is wholly other, merciful and mighty. He is wholly other, forgiving and punishing. God is set apart from everything that is unholy, because He cannot tolerate sin. Joshua aimed to prevent Israel from making an emotionally charged decision.

Joshua knew how fickle Israel had been through the years. He was telling their story, his story, as a crucial part of His-story and their past failure to obey and their failure to rid themselves of idols did not bode well for their future obedience. Joshua knew Israel's repentance would not be sincere and their service to God would not be genuine.

The people of Israel continued to contend with him. They promised to serve the Lord (Joshua 24:21). Joshua eventually acquiesced and said they were their own witnesses to choosing God (24:22). Joshua challenged them to remember they heard themselves with their own ears and would be prosecutors of themselves if they did not live out their commitment to serve the Lord. Vows are not meant to be broken: vows are meant to be kept. God says it is best not to make a vow if we do are not going to keep it (Ecclesiastes 5:5).

Knowing Israel's history, Joshua's warning, and the people's response, one cannot help but wonder how Israel could soon forget the loving kindnesses and tender mercies of their God and fall into diverse temptations and idolatry. Israel's history is filled with disobedience and a refusal to serve the Lord. She is an unfaithful bride to a perfect husband. She is an ungrateful child to a faithful parent. She is an obstinate participant in God's holy plan.

God knows the heart of His people and knows we can be sincere in what we say when the threatening moment is not near. However, when the tension has mounted and the threat is standing before us, believers become like Peter, who in the safety of the upper room made the great commitment to never deny the Lord but weakened in that commitment as he stood in the courtyard of the high priest's residence. There, Peter denied the Lord three times because of the possibility of human punishment he would receive if he did confess his true relationship to Jesus (Luke 22:54-62).

Believers do not have the greatest track record of keeping our commitment to God when the pressure is on and temptation is before us. Thank God for making a way of reconciliation. **Jesus is the greater Joshua who calls believers to a renewal of worship to God through the power of the Holy Spirit.**

The Israelites would have been better served if they had said, "As the Lord helps us, we will worship the Lord." So will we; however, we have the Holy Spirit and must cultivate obedience from hearts of love and gratitude. Good intentions are not good enough. We need and have been empowered with strength that is beyond our strength. We have the indwelling Holy Spirit (Romans 8:9).

The Israelites accepted Joshua's sobering warning. Once again, Joshua told them to get rid of their foreign gods, which were presently among them, and turn their hearts to the Lord, the God of their fathers Abraham, Isaac, and Jacob (Joshua 24:23). The fathers were not perfect, but their hearts were faithful: they put off sin, struggled with sin, and put on obedience through faith. This is Pauline language. Paul admonished the Roman Christians in Romans 13:11-13 to put off darkness and put on light. There is no room for compromise in Christian living (Revelation 3:14-19). God chose lowly Israel and is faithful to her as He blesses all nations through her. He expects the same dedication, determination, and attestation from believers. We must put away sin and put on righteousness.

Jesus told the story of a house inhabited by a demon. The demon was evicted and the house was cleaned and garnished. However, the house remained empty and unoccupied. The devil, after staying in the dry places, sought residence in the empty house again and brought seven more demons to reside in it. The last state of the house was worse than the first

(Matthew 12:43-45). Putting away idol gods must be accompanied by putting on faithfulness and service to the Lord. It cannot be an act; it must be worship.

Reaffirm God's Faithfulness

The congregation finally understood how serving the Lord is inextricably connected to obeying the Lord. They promised to worship God and obey Him (Joshua 24:24). They committed to keep obeying and worshiping. Believers do not give their right hand to the preacher and then go sit down and wait for glory. No! We work while it is day because the night will come. Our confession and choice to live for Jesus establishes a promise.

Joshua drew up a covenant, a statute, and an ordinance with Israel at historic Shechem. He wrote the words of their commitment in the book of the law of God. He took a large stone and placed it and the written document under the oak tree by the sanctuary of the Lord. The stone would serve as "state's evidence," or a prosecuting attorney, against Israel in the future if and when Israel denied their God and turned to serve idol gods.

Stones anticipate value in a people's posterity. Stones are very significant in the history of Israel and even of the church. Jesus is the Stone the builders rejected and became the Chief Cornerstone (Psalm 118:22). The stone at the garden tomb in Jerusalem was rolled away, revealing the empty borrowed tomb, for Jesus is our risen Savior. Its removal reminds believers of God's almighty power.

On that day, Joshua reaffirmed the covenant between God and Israel and gave the benediction. The people went home to their own inherited territory mindful of God's faithfulness to promises even though they were faithless in their service. Just as Joshua, in his old age, recounted God's faithfulness to His people, believers must be intentional about sharing the goodness of the Lord. **Whether we count our blessings or recount them as we witness to someone who needs to hear the testimony of Jesus, we must include God's faithfulness to keep His promises.**

Joshua, God's Servant, Is Dead

Joshua is buried in the homestead of Timnath-serah, the place of his inheritance (Joshua 24:30). Israel was faithful in serving God throughout all the years of Joshua's leadership. There was not one incident of Israel breaking its covenant with God through an idolatrous act. Furthermore, Joshua's leadership influenced Israel even after Joshua's death. Israel continued to remain faithful throughout the administrative leadership of the elders who served with Joshua and who witnessed the mighty works of God done on Israel's behalf.

Other Servants of God Die

God's faithfulness does not end with His servant's death. There is a trinity of burials in this chapter—Joshua, Joseph's bones, and Eleazer, son of Aaron—which approximate in three persons what Christ simultaneously embodies within Himself—prophet, priest, and king. The book of Joshua is the first of the Former Prophets. As such, Joshua can be seen as a prophet. Like Joshua, Jesus is a type of prophet. Human prophets only speak the word of God; however, Jesus is the Word of God.

In this chapter, Eleazar, the high priest who was the son of the first high priest, Aaron, died. Jesus is a type of priest. Human priests bring an offering for the people to God and intercede for the people to God. **But Jesus is the offering for the sacrifice, and He is our High Priest who has ascended into heaven and intercedes on our behalf (Hebrews 4:14-16).**

Joseph, who died in Egypt, was interred in the promised land. He commanded his people not to leave his bones in Egypt. His bones were carried to and buried in the promised land. **Joseph was a type of ruler within a domain, but Jesus is the King of kings and Lord of lords (Revelation 19:16).**

Jesus simultaneously embodies all three of these offices and holds the three offices in tension. God buries His workers but never His work. Joshua, Eleazar, and Joseph all died. **Christ—prophet, priest, and king— died once, never to die again. He reigns forever and ever more. God is faithful to establish His word, His promise and His purpose.**

One day, Jesus Christ will raise Joshua, a prophet type, Eleazar, a priestly type, and Joseph, a kingly type, from the dead, for He is the resurrection who puts death to death. They will be resurrected to worship the One who is the faithful prophet, holiest priest, and King of kings. One day, in the New Jerusalem, they will walk the streets of gold in the homeland of their souls. One day, believers will worship with all the saints, because Jesus, the greater Joshua, calls believers to a renewal of worship to God through the power of the Holy Spirit.

Those faithful servants will hear, "Well done!" Well done for persevering through tough times. Well done for running on through the rain. Well done for learning and recounting the history of the ancestors of our faith. Well done for studying the Word made understandable through the Spirit. Well done for teaching others the way to the cross. Well done, good and faithful servant, well done! The pronouncement will be made in the Land of No More—no more sorrow, no more pain, no more suffering, and no more tears. We will rejoice! Our God is faithful to His promises!

A CLOSER LOOK

Meditate on the Word

Psalm 116:15 says, "The death of His faithful ones is valuable in the LORD's sight." The book of Joshua demonstrates this truth as this book begins with the death of God's servant—one who served Him well, though obviously human in his imperfections.

The book of Joshua ends with a burial record of saints instrumental in the story; however, it also ends with a statement portending to the faithlessness of Israel: "Israel worshiped the LORD throughout Joshua's lifetime and during the lifetimes of the elders who outlived Joshua and who had experienced all the works the LORD had done for Israel" (Joshua 24:31). How could God's commands in the Shema help protect the spiritual legacy of believers (Deuteronomy 6:4-9)? How does the Word encourage believers to share their family's faith history to help descendants serve the Lord?

Faith Matters

A strong faith is the hallmark of outstanding Christians, but many outstanding Christians have wavered in their faith.

Check out these passages revealing faith role models at their lowest moments. Connect the passage to the challenge that caused one's faith to waver.

SPECIAL CIRCUMSTANCES	CHALLENGES TO FAITH
Exodus 3:11	Illness
Judges 6:13	Death
1 Kings 19:1-5	Physical danger
Matthew 8:26	Fitness for leadership
Matthew 14:28-33	Distrust in God's power
Matthew 17:14-20	Risk to reputation or livelihood
Matthew 26:28-34	Environmental threats
Matthew 26:69-75	Lack of authority
Luke 7:19; John 14:1-2	Doubting God's care or love
John 20:25	Concern for material resources

Circle the challenge(s) that most test your faith, and finish this simple prayer below:

God, whenever I am _____

_____

_____, I will trust in You.

Application Questions

1. Why is it important to know your spiritual history, biblical history, and church history? When is it wise to keep personal spiritual history private?

2. When have you made promises to God that you intended to keep but found it difficult to do so? How did you respond? What did you learn from the experience?

3. On what basis was Israel to fear the Lord and worship Him? On what basis are we to fear the Lord and worship Him?

4. What is your most significant takeaway from the book of Joshua?

ABOUT THE AUTHORS

Robert Smith, Jr. (Ph.D., The Southern Baptist Theological Seminary) serves as Profess
of Christian Preaching and holds the Charles T. Carter Baptist Chair of Divinity at Bees
Divinity School. An ordained Baptist minister, he served as pastor of the New Missi
Missionary Baptist Church in Cincinnati, Ohio for twenty years. He earned his Ph.D. whi
serving as pastor.

Dr. Smith has written the books, *Doctrine That Dances: Bringing Doctrinal Preachi*
and Teaching to Life, *The Oasis of God: From Mourning to Morning—Biblical Insights fro*
Psalms 42 and 43 and *Christ-Centered Exposition Commentary: Exalting Jesus in Joshua.*

Dr. Smith has spoken at more than 150 universities, colleges, and seminaries in th
United States and abroad. His research interests include the place of passion in preachir
the literary history of African American preaching, Christological preaching, and theo
gies of preaching. Dr. Smith has contributed essays and articles to various books, magazine
and commentaries. At Beeson, Dr. Smith teaches Christian Preaching and other elective
in homiletics. He and his wife, Dr. Wanda Taylor-Smith, Ph.D., are the parents of fo
adult children (two in heaven) and eight grandchildren

Kima Jude wrote the activities for this Personal Study Guide. She is a member of Th
Oaks Baptist Church in Grand Prairie, Texas, where she leads the women's ministry an
where her husband Barry serves as pastor. Kima has a bachelor's degree in journalism fror
Marshall University and had an early career as a newspaper reporter followed by a fre
lance writing career. She has written for several Christian publications, including Lifeway
January Bible Study and several *Explore the Bible* group plans.

She is employed full-time at a local university in the Dallas-Fort Worth region directin
foundation relations and writing proposals. She and her husband are the parents of fou
young adult children and three young grandchildren. She looks forward to helping then
discover the wonder of the Bible.

ALSO AVAILABLE

An item related to teaching this Personal Study Guide is the *Joshua: The Faithfulness of Go*
(January Bible Study 2025) *Leader Guide* (item number: 005848439). The Leader Guide
includes commentary, teaching plans, and a redeemable code for a digital download with
additional helps.